CONTENTS

ESSAYS FROM THE EDGE

ESSAYS FROM THE EDGE

FIFTY YEARS OF MOUNTAIN WRITING

DENNIS GRAY

Foreword by
JOHN PORTER

Edited by
CATHERINE MOOREHEAD

Bâton Wicks, Sheffield
www.adventurebooks.com

Essays from the Edge
Dennis Gray

First published in 2025 by Bâton Wicks, an imprint of Vertebrate Publishing.
VERTEBRATE PUBLISHING
Omega Court, 352 Cemetery Road, Sheffield S11 8FT, United Kingdom.
www.adventurebooks.com

Front cover: Alpamayo, in the Cordillera Blanca, Peruvian Andes. © wayak/Shutterstock.
Back cover: *Lyskamm, Castor & Pollux* (1849) by Sir John Ruskin (1819–1900) © Alpine Club.
Individual photography as credited.

This book is a work of non-fiction based on the life of Dennis Gray. The author has stated
to the publishers that, except in such minor respects not affecting the substantial
accuracy of the work, the contents of the book are true.

A CIP catalogue record for this book is available from the British Library.

ISBN: 978-1-898573-59-3 (Paperback)
ISBN: 978-1-898573-60-9 (Ebook)

Bâton Wicks is committed to printing on paper from sustainable sources.

MIX
Paper | Supporting
responsible forestry
FSC® C013604

Printed and bound by CPI Group (UK), Croydon CR0 4YY.

For my family, who have always supported me.

FOREWORD

I will start with a short story, one that Dennis himself might have written as an entry to one of his intelligent, wide-ranging and insightful essays. Like many of his essays, the story begins five decades ago, in a time when communication with friends was normally first-hand. There was no anti-social media, and things seemed to happen with a degree of serendipity and magic that has fled the modern world.

I was hitch-hiking back to Leeds from the Lakes. I had been waiting a while in Ingleton for the next lift. Down the road, I saw a large blue Russian sedan approaching. It pulled up in front of me as I lowered my extended thumb and grabbed my rucksack. A window rolled down and I saw the car packed with scruffy climbers and their gear. At the wheel was Dennis. Like Dennis, I was part of the Leeds climbing fraternity in the 1970s, a community which seems to have gained some legendary status these days.

'Hi John. I'm really sorry, but there is no room even for one more. But what are you doing next weekend? There's a Polish exchange coming to Plas y Brenin. I need one more person to host them, with the Burgesses and Pete Boardman. Fancy a week at the Brenin and some climbing with some Polish aces?'

'Sure,' I replied.

'That's sorted then. See you there Friday evening.'

That brief and unexpected encounter led to lifelong friendships and groundbreaking climbs in the Himalaya for Alex MacIntyre and me. Thank you, Dennis.

Others can tell similar stories. Dennis was a nexus and a locus for connections in the climbing world. Many of the essays reveal this, a compendium of encounters with remarkable people – Royal Robbins, Claude Barbier, John Syrett and Roger Baxter-Jones. A bit of the Leeds story is told in essays like 'Whisper the Wind', and in the Allan Austin interview.

Perhaps even more intriguing and revealing are the essays on Joe Brown and Don Whillans. These cover the early days of these exceptional climbers, as well as the stories of the Rock and Ice and the Bradford Lads. At times, there is a violent edge to these stories that characterised the hard men from the northern working classes. Dennis Gray writes of these men with the eye of someone who has studied psychology.

Dennis is also as an eclectic art and social historian. His essays cover a wide range of mountain culture topics. Those about Leslie Stephen, Gary Snyder, several mountain painters and, unexpectedly, Belgium, are a delight to read, and reread if you have come across them on *Footless Crow* or in the *Alpine Journal*. His essay on the Olympics and concerns about competition climbing will be shared by almost all mountaineers.

Dennis's essays are a testament to a life lived for the mountains, from his teenage years of truancy from school to go climbing, to his masterful management of the British Mountaineering Council at a time when adventure and risk were forces that sent us to the mountains, not contracts and the quest for medals.

So, thank you again Dennis. I look forward to seeing this wonderful collection on my shelf.

JOHN PORTER

EDITOR'S PREFACE

It has been a privilege and something of an honour to have edited these essays covering one of British mountaineering's most exciting periods by one of its greatest and most durable exponents. In these essays, you will see Dennis Gray the climber, the diplomat, the aesthete, the student of esoterica, the writer, the social critic and the most individualistic yet clubbable of men.

The essays range correspondingly widely, in geography, in people, in themes and in ideas. The opinions are clear-cut and substantiated, firm in their clarity yet not objectionably aggressive.

I'm delighted to be associated with these fascinating records of our history, not just for the people and ideas but in finding out aspects of lives not previously recorded.

One note: heights are sometimes given in metres and sometimes in feet. This is deliberate: some of the essays read more harmoniously when feet are used; others read better using metres; some read best when the two are mixed.

Any reader anxious about imposing homogeneity should convert feet to metres by dividing feet by 3.048; conversely, multiply metres by the same number to arrive at feet.

CATHERINE MOOREHEAD

PEOPLE

1

SIR LESLIE STEPHEN (1832–1904)

'Fleetest of foot of the whole Alpine brotherhood ... '

— EDWARD WHYMPER

Britain is almost unique in the number of its climbing clubs, unlike other countries where the sport has a major presence such as France, Italy or Germany. Almost every city in the UK has its own climbing club. There are also the long-established organisations which draw their membership nationally: the Scottish Mountaineering Club, the Climbers' Club, the Fell and Rock Climbing Club and the Alpine Club. The British Mountaineering Council has 280 clubs in its membership, while the Mountaineering Council of Scotland has 160. How did this come about? It really has its origins during the Victorian era, when so many organisations were formed and the world's first mountaineering club, the Alpine Club, was founded in 1857. The men – and they were all men in what was then still a most patriarchal society – who were responsible were all from the upper or professional classes. They had the income and leisure to follow what was then seen as a new sport, a new, challenging activity in which they believed themselves to be the experts.

Sir Leslie Stephen (1832–1904). © Alpine Club

It was a golden era, for many of the peaks in the Alps were still unclimbed. The public's interest was aroused by Albert Smith, in the Egyptian Hall, Piccadilly. Thousands of people attended his 2,000 presentations of his illustrated ascent of Mont Blanc, beginning in 1862 and running for six years.

One of the earliest mountaineers to join the Alpine Club was Leslie Stephen, the year after it was formed. He was already a mountaineer who, with the Mathews brothers and their cousin, had pioneered ascents in Austria and North Italy. He was educated at Eton and Trinity Hall, Cambridge, where he had also been ordained as a priest.

At school he had been somewhat sickly and physically weak but at Cambridge he took up rowing. This built up his physique and he started to visit the Alps. His first ascents from 1858 to 1871 stand out, especially in the Valais and Oberland, and mark him out as one of the outstanding early pioneers.

He did not always win favour with his fellow alpinists: they believed his writings gave his guides too much praise and too much credit for his successes. Melchior Anderegg, born near Meiringen and lauded as the 'King of the Guides', was one such. In 2014, a statue of Anderegg and his adventurous 'Herr' was unveiled in that town.

I suppose Stephen's success in completing the Eigerjoch in 1859 and the Jungfraujoch in 1862 made his fellow Alpine Club members aware that a new force was in the membership. The number of first ascents he was to make over the next decade or so highlighted this: Mont Blanc from St Gervais, the Schreckhorn, Zinalrothorn, Alphubel, Monte Disgrazia, Bietschhorn, Rimpfischhorn and Mont Mallet. He made many second ascents, such as the Weisshorn, as well as many other successful climbs. He was elected vice president of the Alpine Club from 1863 to 1865 and president from 1866 to 1868.

In 1862, he abandoned being a clergyman; he later resigned his position at Cambridge, his fellowship depending on this. Eventually, he was to publish a book on this change in belief, *An Agnostic's Apology and Other Essays,* confessing he had never really believed in the Christian message, having been swayed by his family, evangelicals of the Clapham Sect. His father had been the Under-Secretary of State for the Colonies, for which public service he had been knighted.

Stephen moved to London, and from then became a journalist and editor of some renown, initially contributing to the *Saturday Review* and the *Pall Mall Gazette*. Then, in 1865, occurred the accident after the first ascent of the Matterhorn when four of the party were killed on the descent. Alan Lyall's impressive book of almost 700 pages gives full details of this, especially the aftermath: the enquiry, the main figures involved and the media reaction. I do not think any event in mountaineering history has received such coverage; even the monarch was reported to have commented as one of those who died was distantly related.

Much of the media coverage initially was hostile, so much so that Whymper, the sole survivor of the amateur climbers, had to defend himself and write a full account of the disaster in the *Times*. Stephen, who was at that time vice president of the Alpine Club, spoke up for the sport, and defended the role of the senior guide who, to save his own skin, was accused of either cutting the rope or purposely using a weak one.

In 1871, two books appeared which had a large effect on the subsequent development of mountaineering. Edward Whymper published *Scrambles Amongst the Alps,* which included his many attempts to climb the Matterhorn and his eventual success, clouded by the accident on the descent, and *The Playground of Europe* by Leslie Stephen, both of which became instant mountaineering classics and played a part in popularising the activity. The first of these ran to five editions in little more than a decade; both books are still in print.

In 1868, Stephen became editor of the *Alpine Journal.* He was well suited to such a role, his knowledge of the Alpine ranges being probably unsurpassed at that time in Britain: in 1861, he had translated from the German the bestselling, in that country, book which also widely covered many of the less-visited areas: *The Alps,* by Hermann Alexander von Berlepsch. This may have led Stephen to make the first ascent of Monte Disgrazia. Most of the volumes of the *Alpine Journal* which he edited are available on the internet.

He was an early enthusiast for winter ascents, but he made it obvious that he took a very serious view of the dangers inherent in mountaineering, besides the enjoyment and challenge of the sport. Many of the early pioneers who had become friends or rope mates with him suffered serious accident or death.

During the Victorian period, the Alpine Club gained in numbers and influence. Some of those who joined were enthusiasts for mountain scenery, and commented on this, but preferred to view rather than climb to summits; John Ruskin, Matthew Arnold and the well-known publisher John Murray – Byron was one of the poets whom he published – were among those.

Stephen became editor at this time of the *Cornhill Magazine*; the writers for that organ were among those who were to become household names: Robert Louis Stevenson, Thomas Hardy and William Makepeace Thackeray. Stephen married one of the latter's daughters, known to everybody by the nickname 'Minny', who bore him one child, Laura. Cruelly, Minny died while pregnant when Laura was still young.

Stephen is now best known as the founding editor and contributor to the *Dictionary of National Biography,* many of the volumes of which he edited. This incredible academic work is still being updated and published by Oxford University Press and is referred to daily, particularly in our university and public libraries. The original publisher was the same as the *Cornhill Magazine*, which explains Stephen's involvement in the whole project, an editorship which was to lead, among his other works, to a knighthood.

After the death of his first wife, Stephen eventually married a close friend of his wife, a widow who also had three children. They would go on to have a further four children, two of whom were to become more famous than he. One can imagine the noisy atmosphere at his house in Hyde Park Gate, now a blue plaque site, with so many children growing up there. He did employ several maids, however, to look after this brood.

With such domestic demands and the sadness at the loss of his first wife, as well as his editorial work, his involvement in the world of mountaineering became limited. But every Sunday, with like-minded friends, he took what became legendary long walks over the South Downs, and further afield. His band of ramblers became known as 'The Tramps'; twenty to thirty miles were often covered on their outings. In a history of walking in this country, *Ramble On,* by Sinclair McKay, full details about The Tramps can be found. What is memorable about this is a list of all who took part in these walks – everyone from those who made their living by their pen, to judges and Queen's Counsels.

Stephen died in 1904, but the family's fame was to rise and rise, since two of his daughters eclipsed his memory. Vanessa married Quentin Bell and moved to Bloomsbury, where she was joined by Virginia, who had married Leonard Woolf. This was the beginning of what became known as the Bloomsbury set, which included E.M. Forster, Lytton Strachey, John Maynard Keynes and many other prominent figures of that time.

Vanessa Bell and Virgina Woolf in their respective fields are admired for their achievements: Vanessa in the field of art, particularly abstractions; Virginia is one of the most famous novelists worldwide, a leader of modernist fiction and an archetypal figure in the feminist movement. I was surprised to learn that her biggest fan base is now in the USA. Her father is very much caricatured in her most famous work, *To the Lighthouse*: he is the Mr Ramsay who leads his family on an adventurous holiday to the Isle of Skye.

Leslie Stephen was very much a product of his time, when everybody had beards like the Taliban, and Victorians of his background did not worry too much about their privileged existence. But they did leave a society that was capable of change. The Alpine Club is a prime example of this: to be a member now depends on one's climbing record, not social standing. Sir Leslie Stephen set the sport on the path for which today's climbing fraternity should be grateful.

This article first appeared on *Footless Crow* in September 2021.

2

THE ROUND OF EXISTENCE
AND MARCO PALLIS

'Poor is the pupil who does not surpass his master.'

— LEONARDO DA VINCI

I began researching and subsequently contacting a wide range of individuals with specialist knowledge about the life of Marco Pallis, motivated in this by rereading two books from my earliest climbing days: *Helvellyn to Himalaya* (1940) by F. Spencer Chapman, and *Let's Go Climbing!* (1941) by Colin Kirkus. Within their pages is the story of how both made it to climb in the Himalaya through the inspiration and organising abilities of Marco Pallis, Kirkus in 1933 and Chapman in 1936. The climbs they made on these expeditions were among the most important ascents by British climbers in that decade.

Marco Pallis was born in Liverpool in 1895, into a wealthy Anglo-Greek family. His father, Alexandros, was by that date the head of the Ralli trading house in Liverpool, big in importing cotton and in its operations within the Orient, including banking. He had married the daughter of one of the principals, Julia Ralli, in 1881. But Alexandros was also one of the foremost Greek scholars of his era, translating the *Iliad*, *Antigone* and the *New Testament* into modern Greek (all published by Oxford University

Press). The latter caused riots in Athens in 1901, as it was banned by the Greek Orthodox Church. I guess it is rare for such a scholar to be a successful businessman, but he was to become one of the richest men in Liverpool, impressive for someone who had needed to drop out of education in Athens in 1869, to travel from there to Manchester to seek employment. He obtained a post with Ralli, then based in Manchester and from where he moved to Bombay in 1889, to finally settle in Liverpool in 1894, and to become a British subject. While in Bombay he wrote a book of poetry, *Little Songs for Children,* which was popular in the late Victorian era.

Marco was one of five children, three boys and two girls; he was the youngest of the sons and was bundled off to Harrow at a tender age. But when he began to take a keen interest in Roman Catholicism, attending extra lessons with a priest, his parents brought him back to Liverpool and a private tutor. At sixteen, he journeyed to British Guiana to study insects and flora, and the following year he joined the Greek campaign against the invading Ottoman armies in the first Balkan War. During the siege of Ioannina, which is the ancestral home of the Pallis family, he worked at a field hospital in Arta. Returning to the UK, he enrolled at the University of Liverpool to study zoology, but after the first year he moved to entomology. Having grown to physical maturity, he was 5 feet 8 inches in height, with dark hair, rugged features and a lithe physique.

The First World War then intervened; he volunteered with the Salvation Army to work in Serbia, but then he became a translator for the British Army in Macedonia. Unfortunately, this ended badly after he developed malaria and a serious eye infection, and he was shipped out to a hospital in Malta. Once he had recovered, he was commissioned in the Grenadier Guards, specialising as a machine gunner. After some terrible experiences in the trenches, the war ended for him at Cambrai in 1918. In a charge, both his captain and lieutenant were killed, and he found himself the remaining leader until he was shot badly through a knee. Returning to England to convalesce and for rehabilitation, he was warned not to try anything too physically challenging. In fact, one doctor advised that he might never walk properly again. Such worry must have been allayed somewhat by his family passing over a £50,000 inheritance to help him overcome this disability!

It seems that around this date his life really began as a climber, but it also produced the awakening of another interest: he was to make a name as a musician and a composer, yet this also led him into climbing. He had studied music as a boy and had realised his keenest interest was in classical music. In 1920, he was to be found at Haslemere, studying under Dr Arnold Dolmetsch. Because of his influence, he discovered a love of chamber music of the sixteenth and seventeenth centuries and in playing the viola da gamba. Dolmetsch was French; besides being a major influence in reawakening an interest in early music, and being an outstanding musician, he was also a skilled craftsman, making replica copies of violas, recorders and harpsichords. Pallis was so impressed by this ability that he provided the money in 1921 to build a large workshop to undertake such activities.

At Haslemere, two other events occurred that were to have a major influence on Marco. One was meeting his life partner, a fellow musician and composer, Richard Nicholson, ten years his junior and the son of C.E. Nicholson, famous as a yacht designer; the other was a chance meeting with the brother of one of the other students who was a climber. He persuaded Pallis and Nicholson to go climbing with him, and they became hooked on the sport.

Back in Liverpool, the climbing scene was moving into a golden age, from the late 1920s and throughout the 1930s. Just as happened at the end of the 1940s and 1950s after the Second World War, the recovery of the sport from the losses in the 1914–1918 war were to be made up and surpassed by new leaders, bolstered by advances in techniques and equipment. Returning home, Pallis joined Liverpool's Wayfarers, and over the next few years he was to share a rope with some of the most outstanding climbers of that era, such as Menlove Edwards, Ted Hicks, Jake Cooke, A.B. Hargreaves, Ivan Waller and Colin Kirkus.

In 1929, with Hargreaves, he and Nicholson made the third ascent of *Longland's Climb* on Clogwyn Du'r Arddu, and with Kirkus he seconded the first ascent of the *Birthday Crack* on that same cliff. He and Ivan Waller also supported Colin in pioneering the first ascent of the *Mickledore Grooves* on Scafell's East Buttress in 1931, while Bill Stallybrass and Marco seconded Menlove Edwards' first free ascent of the *Central Buttress* on Scafell Crag's main face. These years were to be hyperactive, climbing-wise, for Pallis and Nicholson, attending club meets in the Lake District, the Peak District, Snowdonia and the Scottish Highlands. They also made trips to the Arctic, the Dolomites and the Alps. One of the first such visits came in 1926, to

Saas-Fee, where the highlight was a traverse of the Mischabel. Kirkus's first Alpine season was with Pallis and Bob Frost; the latter, to all who knew him, was so certain of a great climbing future, but his life was to end tragically young in a motorcycle accident.

It seemed the Alps called every year. Wherever Pallis and Nicholson travelled to, there was music: Ted Hicks was a fine singer and others within the Wayfarers' membership would join in.

Pallis was also a keen innovator of equipment and liked testing his ideas in extreme conditions. In the winter of 1929, he and Kirkus bivvied on the summit of Snowdon in sixteen degrees of frost (-9 °C). Marco reported that, 'Colin slept so soundly, I feared he must be dead.' A short while later, he and Nicholson repeated the exercise on the summit of Ben Nevis, but Pallis found this latter outing far less comfortable than the Snowdonia adventure, both of which were to test sleeping bag design. He put down his ideas about equipment development in an article entitled 'Bivouacs', published in the 1933 *Wayfarers' Journal*, suggesting ways to improve lightweight gear for camping: tents, sleeping bags and the design of mountaineering boots. He even suggested a collapsible pee bottle for personal emergencies while camping. He obviously was thinking of the Himalaya and an expedition he was shortly to lead.

In 1931, he was elected a vice president of the Wayfarers, and in 1933 its president. There is an amusing published note by one of his club officers about meetings at Pallis's parents' house. You can imagine by this date they lived in grand style, and by order of Marco's mother, his 'scruffy' climbing friends could only meet in their basement. However, he did show how forward-thinking he was, for he suggested that the climbing clubs should meet and produce a scheme to help poorer younger climbers visit the Alps. He also noted, unlike some other mountaineering commentators of the 1930s, his admiration for the leading continental mountaineers, in the way they trained physically and mentally for major climbs.

He enjoyed a successful Alpine season in the Valais in 1932 with Ted Hicks and Nicholson, ascending among other peaks the Alphubel, the Dom and the Täschhorn. Some of the other alpinists of that era remarked how Pallis's times on many of his ascents were slow, but for a man who just a decade earlier had been informed he might never walk again, his climbs were remarkable, as he was to prove in succeeding years in the Himalaya. Freddie Spencer Chapman, a decorated Second World War soldier, noted,

'Pallis hides a good deal of determination behind his mild manner!' And despite being a 'steady as you go mountaineer', he was elected to the Alpine Club shortly afterwards.

The 1933 Wayfarers' Gangotri expedition, made up of Colin Kirkus, Dr Charles Warren, Richard Nicholson and Ted Hicks, which Marco organised and led, must have been one of the happiest and most successful of its time, enlivened while marching to a Gangotri glacier base by Pallis and Nicholson performing in the evenings on their viols, to the amazement and delight of villagers and porters. Several peaks were ascended by different partnerships, but the standout climb was the first ascent of Bhagirathi III (6,454 metres), via its south ridge, by Kirkus and Warren. This entailed some high-altitude free rock climbing, led by Kirkus at a standard hardly achieved in the Himalaya before that date.

The first half of the expedition being completed, for Hicks and Kirkus needed to travel home and back to work, Nicholson, Warren and Pallis trekked north towards the Tibetan border to avoid the arrival of the monsoon. There, they settled on a mountain, Riwo Pargyul North (6,791 metres), successfully climbed by Warren and Pallis. (This massif, comprising three peaks, including the highest in Himachal Pradesh at 6,816 metres, is most commonly referred to as Reo Purgyil, sometimes Leo Pargial, and many variations of those names. See *Himalayan Journal* 48 for more detail on its confusing nomenclature, a consequence of colonial surveying.) It was this journey to the border, and meeting Tibetans, that awakened Marco's interest in that country, its peoples and Tibetan Buddhism. It should be noted that all the climbs on the 1933 expedition were achieved without porter support, a source of pride to all those who took part.

The Wayfarers held a meet each Easter in Fort William, with winter climbing on Ben Nevis being the *raison d'être* for the gathering. On occasion, many 'irregulars' joined in, including Jack Longland, Graham MacPhee, the compiler of the first climbing guide to the mountain, and in 1934 Maurice Linnell. Climbing with Colin Kirkus, they set off up the Castle on Carn Dearg, which I know from an ascent I made in 1953 as a teenager is a notorious avalanche trap, especially after heavy snowfall. Maurice and Colin were victims of such conditions, resulting in a serious accident in which Linnell was killed and Kirkus badly injured. One can never know what might have been, for both men were among the most outstanding climbers of their era, and though Kirkus survived, it marked the end of his bold pioneering. Nevertheless, after a long period of recovery he returned to climbing, but it seems that his desire for new routing was sated. It must have been traumatic for Pallis as the Wayfarers' president to deal with this event, but his kindly and caring nature was much to the fore and appreciated.

In 1936, another Himalayan expedition was organised by Pallis, this time to Sikkim and the Kangchenjunga area, with Simvu (6,811 metres) as the major objective, but with other nearby mountains as possibilities. The party was made up of Jake Cooke, of *Main Wall* on Cyrn Las fame, Freddie Spencer Chapman, Dr Robert Roaf and Richard Nicholson. Simvu turned out to be a much harder mountain than expected: they were stopped high on the peak by a difficult pitch. Writing about this, Chapman explained it was a vertical corner, which once negotiated was blocked by a twenty-foot-high band of extremely steep ice. With a lot of difficulty, this was led by Pallis, cutting handholds and footholds in the ice wall. Chapman confessed, 'I would not have liked it much without the support of a rope!' With that climbed, and having gained an easy ridge, Nicholson, Cooke, Pallis and Chapman were convinced they had the main difficulties behind them and the summit in view. But they were to be stopped on easy ground by a huge crevasse. While searching for a way to cross this, first it started to snow, then a blizzard set in. Descending through this was a trial, and with no let-up in the adverse conditions, they had to abandon Simvu.

Pallis had hoped to visit Tibet on this expedition, but his application was rejected, and so he, Nicholson and Roaf trekked north over high passes into Ladakh, while Cooke, Chapman and Jock Harrison, who had by good fortune joined the other two when his own companion had retreated due to illness, made ascents of the technically straightforward Sphinx Peak (6,970 metres) but finished with the more difficult Fluted Peak (6,085 metres).

Ladakh was everything that Pallis had dreamed of, with its monasteries, its lamas, its Buddhism and its Tibetan peoples. Both he and Nicholson converted to Buddhism. Pallis explained this spiritual journey in a book which has become a classic of its genre, *Peaks and Lamas,* first published in 1939. This has deeply affected many of those who have studied this work – everyone from Gary Snyder and Philip Glass to Allen Ginsberg. It has appeared in English editions in the USA, India and the UK, and has been translated just as widely. It is a most unusual work as mountaineering literature. It tells the story of the two climbing expeditions, and it contains some lucid and sensitive travel writing, but underpinning both of these is an explanation of Tibetan Buddhism's history, precepts and practice. It is a difficult read, challenged by abstract doctrines that for most are difficult to grasp, although the American writer Wendell Berry wrote after reading it, that, 'I find no other writer on Buddhism surpassing him.' I counted ten editions published so far of *Peaks and Lamas*; Pallis is certainly one of those who introduced Tibetan Buddhism to many in the West.

Pallis visited the Alps again in 1938, climbing with Jake Cooke. They ascended a host of peaks, including the Obergabelhorn, Wellenkuppe and the Breithorn, but the darkening storm of war caught up with such idyllic outings: Cooke was to perish a short while later at Dunkirk. Pallis retreated to Liverpool and in the war worked during the day at the Citizens Advice Bureau, and in the evenings took on special constable duties in reaction to the massive air raids visited on the city. Surprisingly, though, being by then forty-eight years old, he was called to appear before a tribunal for conscientious objectors in Liverpool's St George's Hall on 1 October 1943. His objection to military service was upheld on account of his pacific Buddhist beliefs.

In 1947, he and Nicholson were at last able to visit Tibet, where they travelled widely through the Tsang area. At Shigatse, they were 'ordained' in a ceremony at the Tashilhunpo monastery, the seat of the Panchen Lama and one of the four major sites of the Gelugpa sect (there being three others, all older: Nyingmapa, Kagyudpa, Sakyapa), the same sect as the Dalai Lama. Both he and Nicholson liked their Tibetan names, Pallis being known as Thubden Tendzin. By that time, Pallis was fluent in the language, writing a short book in Tibetan which attempted to warn of how he saw trouble looming in accepting the dangers of modern civilisation, and a possible outside incursion into a society which, though he recognised as primitive, he had found spiritual, traditional and serene. He and Nicholson then retreated to Kalimpong, where they lived for nearly four years. Kalimpong was at that time a centre of literary and cultural activities as well as a refuge for many of those who were forced to leave Tibet after China's occupation. Pallis became active in the Tibet Society, the first support group created to aid the Tibetan exiles. One of the surprising items of furniture Marco owned in his bungalow at Kalimpong was a harpsichord, which often astonished visitors.

Returning to Britain in 1951, he picked up on his previous life, particularly early music. He reestablished an ensemble, the English Consort of Viols, which he had first formed in the 1930s. He also developed his ability as a composer, and by the 1960s he had become a professor at the Royal Academy of Music, a post he held for over a decade, with his work there being recognised as worthy of an honorary fellowship. His 'String Quartet in F#' became a performance piece for the Salomon Quartet. With the Consort, he toured widely in the UK and the USA, with the *New York Times* declaring a sell-out event in New York in 1962, 'A solid musical delight.' The Consort released three records, of which *Music of the English Home* is accepted as a classic of early music.

Pallis kept to his Buddhist beliefs, writing two further books on that subject: *The Way and the Mountain* (1960) and *Buddhist Spectrum* (1980). He was acknowledged as a major contributor to perennial philosophy, and he became a frequent contributor to *Studies in Comparative Religion,* an academic journal that carried the view that all religions have at their core common 'truths'. Among his fellow writers were Frithjof Schuon, René Guénon, Ananda Coomaraswamy and Aldous Huxley (who wrote a book on this subject). Pallis's writings were published in Italian, French, Spanish and Turkish; he also translated several works by his fellow perennial writers from French into English.

As he moved into an advanced age he continued to write and compose, and at the age of eighty-nine, his 'Nocturne de L'Éphémère' (The Mayfly's Evensong) was performed at the Queen Elizabeth Hall. The audience insisted the composer should appear on stage at the end of the concert, and he received a rousing reception. For many years, he worked on an opera based on the life of Milarepa, a celebrated Tibetan poet and saint, composing the music, writing the libretti and designing the costumes. It remains almost finished, but needs a composer of the stature of Fenton or Britten to do it justice and complete the task. Perhaps someone will take this on.

Pallis died in 1989, aged ninety-three. One of those who paid keenest tribute to his memory was Charles Warren, doctor on the 1936 and 1938 Everest expeditions and a member of Marco's 1933 Gangotri expedition. It read: 'Marco Pallis! A household name among most mountaineers of my generation, a very gentle, gifted and most lovable man.' To those readers who have never been on a climbing expedition, particularly one like the 1933 Gangotri trip, which lasted for over half a year, this is so telling, for normally one might be hard pressed to find a participant so willing to pay such a heartfelt tribute to his leader.

This article first appeared in the 2020 *Alpine Journal.*

3

THE COLD MOUNTAIN POET:
GARY SNYDER

'Who can leap the world's ties
And sit with me among the white clouds?'

— HAN SHAN, POET OF THE TANG DYNASTY

In the late 1960s, I was walking back to Camp 4 in the Yosemite Valley, accompanied by the legendary US climber Chuck Pratt, when we met another outdoor enthusiast walking in the opposite direction towards us. This stranger, unknown to me, was known to Chuck, and they exchanged greetings. I was introduced in that offhand way that climbers think of as sufficient, and we went on our way, eager to reach camp and slake our thirst after a day's climbing in August's intense heat.

Once back in camp, I ventured to ask Chuck who the guy we had met earlier was. 'Oh, he is from the University of California. Many years ago, he worked here in the park, trail building. So he knows a lot about Yosemite and its history.' I had only heard in our introduction that his name was Gary. It was sometime later that I realised that this was Gary Snyder, one of the most famous writers in the States, already with a legendary back story, and a mountaineer of some experience beginning with a very youthful initiation into the sport.

I had been introduced to Gary's writings by one of my own mentors, the late Harold Drasdo, when I was also young. In one of our discussions while bivouacking under Castle Rock in the Lake District, Harold had enthused about an essay he had recently read by Gary about hitch-hiking. As at that time it was our own mode of transport, this was what had caused him to get to grips with this essay: he opined that it was the best such piece of writing he had ever read about the activity, and he recommended me to read it. High praise indeed, for Harold had a critical eye for such literature.

So, from an early age, the name Gary Snyder was known to me, and after our chance meeting in Yosemite Valley I have followed his career with more than a little interest. It is one of the most fascinating life stories that I know of. For he is a poet, essayist, environmentalist, logger, academic, mountaineer, Zen Buddhist, trail builder, fire lookout and much more.

He was born in the San Francisco area in 1930, but following the break-up of his parents' marriage he moved as a schoolboy to Portland, Oregon, where he went to school and eventually college. With other school friends, he started travelling into the countryside, and then as a young teenager started to climb. He joined the Mazamas mountaineering club, based in Portland, and over the next few years he ascended many of the major peaks in the Cascade Mountains, such as Mounts Hood, Baker, Rainier, Shasta, Adams and St Helens. As a fifteen-year-old, while descending off the latter, he learned with horror of the dropping of atomic bombs on Hiroshima and Nagasaki.

By the time he was twenty years old he was a highly experienced mountaineer, but his ascents were accomplished with a brio where he wished,

to develop a fresh mountaineering mind-set that was totally opposed to the notion of conquest. I and the circle I climbed with were extremely critical of what we saw as the hostile Jock, occidental mind-set which was to conquer it ... [we] always thought of mountaineering not as a matter of conquering the mountain, but as a matter of self-knowledge.

He also went on to note that,

my first interest in writing poetry came from the experience of mountaineering. I couldn't find any other way to talk about it.

Snyder studied literature and anthropology at Reed College, and became interested in folklore research: he spent some time at the Warm Springs Indian Reservation in Central Oregon. This experience was to be a major influence on him, drawing on the Indians' songs and poems and feelings about nature and mountain scenery. This experience also marked the beginning of an interest in Buddhism, particularly because of its sympathetic attitudes to nature.

Each winter there was also mountain skiing. He ran around with a group of older ex-ski troopers who called themselves the 'Wolken-Schiebers'.*

After graduating, he obtained a fellowship at Indiana University to study anthropology, but he left and moved to San Francisco to follow his growing interest in Asian culture, languages and poetry. For this he enrolled at the University of California at Berkeley, specialising in ink and wash painting and Tang dynasty poetry. He continued to climb and spent the whole of a summer in Yosemite, working as a trail builder. He studied under Saburō Hasegawa, who introduced him to landscape painting as a meditative practice, and he began work on his most famous poetic work, *Mountains and Rivers Without End,* which he did not complete for forty years. He also embarked on a translation of the 'Cold Mountain' poems, by the legendary eighth-century Chinese recluse Han Shan, whose name in translation simply means 'Cold Mountain'.

No one knows who really wrote these poems, but they are some of the Tang dynasty's most famous; they have been translated into many languages. In Japan they have a similar recognition to Shakespeare in the UK. The Tang dynasty (618–907 CE) was the golden age of Chinese poetry; it is hard-hitting, authentic verse. Here is Snyder's translation of poem number eleven (there are hundreds of them in the sequence):

Spring-water in the green creek is clear
Moonlight on Cold Mountain is white
Silent knowledge – the spirit is enlightened of itself
Contemplate the void: this world exceeds stillness.

During these early years of the 1950s, San Francisco was a gathering

---

* From the German *Wolkenschieber,* 'cloud-pusher', one who finds solace after hardship.

place for poets and a focal point for what became known as the 'Beat' movement. This actually had its origins on the East Coast of the USA with William S. Burroughs, Jack Kerouac and Allen Ginsberg, but it moved west and ended in California along with its leading proponents. Snyder got to know Kerouac through these associations and persuaded him to become, like himself, a fire watcher in the Northern Cascades.

Kerouac was later to recall of their first meeting that unlike the other urban-dwelling, so-called Beats (such as Ginsberg, Lawrence Ferlinghetti and Gregory Corso), outdoorsman Snyder did not look like a 'poet'. My memory of him from my own short introduction was of a physically power-ful, dark and lithe individual of above medium height, with a wispy beard; someone who could have been a lumberjack, which it transpires he has also been, in between courses.

It was in the summer of 1953 that Snyder and Kerouac worked as fire lookouts. This is now the subject of a coffee table book of photographs and text by John Suiter, *Poets on the Peaks* (Counterpoint, 2002). Snyder's lookout was on Sourdough Mountain, and Kerouac's on Desolation Peak. One feels, reading about this now, that the latter took some persuading to take this on, but was converted to the idea by Snyder's mantra that, 'the twin of the active life is the contemplative one'; as a fire lookout for six weeks, one has many hours in which to undertake this!

Amazingly, now, Snyder's activities as a poet interested in Chinese stud-ies, and working as a lookout in the summer months, brought him to the attention of the infamous senator Joseph McCarthy, head of the House Un-American Activities Committee. Snyder was blackballed for not being patriotic enough to work any longer for the US government as a lookout. At least he was in good company, for many of the most outstanding artists and writers of that era suffered a similar fate, from Arthur Miller to Charlie Chaplin.

The experience, however, of working as a lookout led Kerouac to write one of his most famous Beat novels, *The Dharma Bums*. In this, three friends head off to the High Sierra mountains in search of Dharma, or Truth, and to experience the Zen way of life. The climb therein described, up the Matterhorn, is one of the most memorable in American literature. Snyder is the inspiration for the novel's main character, the mountain-climbing, haiku-writing Japhy Ryder. At Snyder's suggestion, the novel

closes with a vision of the aforementioned Han Shan. The work is dedicated to this fabled Tang dynasty poet.

The literary fame of the Beat poets was launched in October 1955 at a
reading in the Six Gallery in San Francisco. While it is Ginsberg's long
poem 'Howl' that is best remembered, Snyder's follow-on contribution 'A
Berry Feast' has also stood the test of time. Most of the Beats were enam-
oured of Eastern religion and psychedelia (way ahead of groups like the
Beatles and other popular artists of the 1960s); for Snyder, it was Zen
Buddhism that was to be his spiritual muse. (Zen is a fusion of Mahayana
Buddhism and Daoism. This latter is a purely Chinese construct, as is Zen,
which is known in China as Chan.) Bidding goodbye to the Beat poets,
Snyder took off in 1956 for Japan, where he enrolled at a monastery in
Kyoto to study Zen, as well as to continue his writing and translating
poetry. His 1957 collection of poems *The Back Country* also includes transla-
tions by him of the now famous Japanese poet Kenji Miyazawa (1896–1933).
Snyder stayed in Japan until 1964, then returned to the USA as a crew
member on an oil freighter.

Once back in the USA, Snyder started work on building his own house
in the northern Sierra mountains and found occasional employment as a
logger, but he never stopped writing and lobbying for wilderness preservation. Over the following decades, he became acknowledged as America's
primary poet-celebrant of the wilderness, a nature poet in the tradition of
Thoreau and Emerson.

From the late 1960s onwards, Snyder's poetry and essays have never
ceased to flow. In 1969 came *Riprap and Cold Mountain Poems;* in 1975 he won
a Pulitzer Prize for his *Turtle Island* collection.* Over the ensuing years he
published over twenty volumes of poetry or essays. Some, like *Turtle Island,*
have been reprinted many times. Other works, such as *Danger on Peaks*
(2004), might be readily identified with by climbers, including as it does
poems of Snyder's own first ascent of Mount St Helens. In 1996, he finally
published his great work *Mountains and Rivers Without End* after forty years
of labour on its contents, winning the Bollingen Prize for Poetry for his
efforts. If he lived in the UK he would now be seen as a national treasure,
loaded as he is with awards including a Guggenheim Foundation

---

* Riprap: a stone cobble laid on steep, slick rock to make a trail for horses in the mountains;
Turtle Island is an indigenous name for North America.

Fellowship, the Shelley Memorial Award, the Bess Hokin Prize, the Levinson Prize for poetry and so much more, including a major award in Japan for a collection of haiku.

His essays are equally notable, especially *The Practice of the Wild* (North Point Press, 1990), a series of ten pieces which are now identified as a central work on the interaction of nature and culture, calling from its pages for an ecological consciousness. He has been described as the poet laureate of deep ecology.

His latest book of poems, *This Present Moment,* was published by Counterpoint in 2015. For many years he was a professor at the University of California, Berkeley, of which he is now an emeritus professor, and he was inducted into the American Academy of Arts and Letters in 1987. The most impressive aspect of all this recognition is that he is still highly regarded by his fellow poets and critics. Not a bad outcome for someone who originally only started writing to express his feelings about his mountaineering experiences.

So, maybe we can claim him as one of our own?

This article first appeared on *Footless Crow* in February 2015.

4

THE BARON: JOE BROWN

'In Langdale's green valley, where the lads are so pally,
As soon as they learn you have food, fags, or dough.
The climber retires, to the barn of Zeke Myers,
Crying ackers and shekels, alive, alive oh!'

— FROM A SONG BY THE BRADFORD LADS

The door of the Wall End barn was pushed open. Outside, it was raining heavily, as it had been doing all that day, and the one preceding it. Into the warm fug created by the number of bodies lying about gossiping, cooking and sleeping, stepped two strangers: one, physically like an ox, tall and well built, the other smaller but of what was then medium height, both of them dark haired, both carrying huge packs and dripping wet. One of the barn regulars ventured a 'hello', wondering where they had come from, imagining they had got so wet walking from Chapel Stile where the midday bus turned off to Coniston.

'Scafell,' was the laconic reply from the ox.

This was 1951. I was fifteen years old, and I guess a bit of a pain as, instead of going to school, I spent a lot of time in the Yorkshire Ramblers' Club library in Leeds, reading journals and climbing books.

Joe Brown. © Trinity Mirror/Mirrorpix

Intrigued, I began to question the newcomers what routes they had done as they unpacked: they had climbed on Esk Buttress and Scafell's East Buttress. This seemed incredible to me in the conditions, but my questioning was obviously so annoying that I was grabbed, bundled into a bag which was tied up with slings, carried outside and placed on top of a wall on the Blea Tarn Road. I was scared stiff, but despite the sharp stones of the wall sticking into me I daren't move in case I fell off.

After what seemed a long time, my jailers reappeared. The ox demanded to know if I had learned to shut up, and through the rain and the cold I admitted I had, at which point they carried me back inside the barn, cut me loose and even made me a brew. To be fair to my young self, I was climbing with Peter Greenwood, Harold Drasdo and, infrequently at that time, Arthur Dolphin. None of them would have had the temerity to be on Scafell in such weather. I subsequently learned that the shorter of the two, Joe Brown, was the best bad-weather climber I would ever tie on with, and that his partner, Slim Sorrell, was his perfect foil, being as I have intimated above, a truly strong man. Thus began two of my friendships which lasted until their respective deaths: Joe in his bed at eighty-nine; Slim in a macabre sequence of events that ended with his murder at the age of forty-seven.

A few weeks later, I met Ronnie Moseley and Ray Greenall, also at Wall End. They told of the formation of a new climbing club, the Rock and Ice, and that both Joe and Slim had joined. My loyalty was then to the Bradford

Lads, just a loose-knit group of climbers who originally got together by visiting the West Yorkshire outcrops. It was never a club, but later I learned that was what Joe really believed in. It was his close friendships with many of those involved that meant he did sign up, and with his membership the Rock and Ice became legendary, although within their ranks they had other climbers who were almost as adept.

I kept in touch with Ron and learned that Slim was organising a Rock and Ice bus trip to Glen Coe at Easter 1952, so I badgered him and was on board when it set off from the centre of Manchester late one evening. My seat companion was Don Whillans and I had never then met anyone so acerbic. I had met him once before as I jogged down the Llanberis track having just completed my first route on Cloggy. 'Bloody stuck up,' was the epithet he hurled at me on that occasion as I passed him, terrified by his aggression. I was pleased that more gentle souls were on board, including Joe and his then girlfriend, Mavis Jolley. She had been to school with him, and she told me later he was known as 'that small Chinese boy'. Joe's schooling finished at fourteen when the Nazis bombed that building flat. He was apprenticed to Archie, a one-man property-repairing business.

This must have been the slowest bus trip ever to brave Shap, for it kept on breaking down and it took most of the four-day holiday to reach our objective. Brown and Whillans spent what time was left exploring the then unclimbed Creag a' Bhancair, while I joined in an ascent of the Clachaig Gully, which was rather more like swimming than rock climbing. An amusing aside: sometime after this I was climbing with Pat Walsh while we made the second ascent of *Carnivore* on Bhancair. I told Joe I had found the route bloody hard. 'You must have been off form,' he replied. 'That crag's full of big holds.' Brown was not easily impressed.

By 1952, the Rock and Ice legend was the talk of the climbing fraternity. There were no magazines, no internet; their standing spread by word of mouth, although some of the detail of their new routes was published rather belatedly in the long defunct BMC publication *Mountaineering*. It is a truth that after the Second World War it was the working-class climbers, mainly from the grime and poverty of the northern cities – the Creagh Dhu in Scotland, the Bradford Lads in the Lake District and the Rock and Ice in Wales – that dominated the sport. There had been working-class climbers before the war, but they had mainly been limited by a six-day working week or unemployment and lack of funding. The long-established clubs, with a mainly middle-class membership, looked askance at this flood of newcomers into a preserve they looked upon as their own. This prompted a riposte from Slim Sorrell: 'When we met some of the members of established clubs at the outcrops they rather cold shouldered us until we started to climb, then they went all sheepish and moved away.'

Petrol rationing had finished in 1950, although food was still couponed. I had found that as a schoolboy climber I was lucky when hitch-hiking, although there were few vehicles on the road. I had kept in touch with the Rock and Ice and joined them for my first visit to the Roaches, where we stayed in a barn close by. On the first evening, I joined in the 'rough' games session. Every member had a speciality, but Joe was the only one who could 'bum skip', literally sitting on the floor and skipping with a short piece of rope. That caused much hilarity.

The next day I was collared by Brown to second him up the *Sloth*. Not long before this visit, he and Whillans had pioneered this fearsome roof climb on the Upper Tier of the crag. They had spun a coin for who should lead, and despite Joe's double-headed penny (a joke around the belief we held at that time), Don won the honour of the first attempt on one of the most famous outcrop climbs of that era. He did not waste the opportunity, and after a bit of a struggle, moving out along the flakes under the roof, he managed to reach some good jams, then hung down and pulled up. Seconding, Joe had not found it technically too demanding, but it rather rankled with him and he wanted to experience an ascent on the lead.

Next morning, I climbed up to the pedestal ledge under the roof while my leader readied himself. I then securely belayed Joe while he climbed up to a feature we called the Cheese Block, around which he draped a sling. He then climbed up and launched himself across the roof, somehow reached round and found good jams, hung down and then, with a heave, was up and out of my sight. The rope went tight between us and I started to climb, easily at first, up to the Cheese Block, but then my problems started as the rope was pulling me off! Remember at that time we tied directly on to it.

Then I recalled how on the first ascent, Don, being small, had managed to wedge himself across the roof, his body fitting into the flakes. I somehow managed to do the same, my difficulty being how I would extricate myself from this position. Suddenly, from below me on the pedestal, came these instructions: 'Reach out your full length – there you will find a jug and stonking jams. Lower on to your arms and pull up.' It was Joe on the pedestal giving the sage advice; he had obviously descended at speed down the easier route on our left. I followed his instructions, although as I climbed the rope remained slack. I imagined somebody else was holding the rope and I kept shouting, 'Take in!' On reaching the top, I was more than surprised to find my rope firmly belayed, but nobody there. Later, when I tried to remonstrate with Joe, he answered cheerfully, 'You were firmly belayed, and you couldn't have fallen far!' Being a senpai of the sensei was a real apprenticeship!

That same year of 1954 I travelled to the Llanberis Pass where I found shelter in the road menders' hut, set under the Cromlech Boulder. There was a mixed group, mainly members of the Rock and Ice, and we had the door of our dwelling firmly shut, with a large boulder stopping anyone we did not want to allow into our midst. Just a few weeks before, one of the Rock and Ice had been arrested by the police for staying there, and we did not wish to suffer the same fate. The weather outside was abysmal and we spent most of that rainy, cold day in our sleeping bags, playing card games. About five o'clock, there came a hammering on the door, and the high-pitched voice we all recognised: 'Let us in!' It was Joe and a companion we knew as G.G. White. They were wet through, and the chorus was:

'Where have you been?'

'Idwal.'

'What on earth did you do there?'

'*Suicide Wall.*'

'You must be joking.'

'No,' answered Brown. 'It was hard.'

'What was it like, G.G.?'

'Bloody hard, like Joe says!'

I doubt whether any other leader then active would have climbed that route in such conditions.

Shortly after, we moved into a club hut because so many of us crowded into the road menders' cabin that it became untenable. Slim decided the time had come for an eating contest: at that time he was the instigator of the wilder activities of the club – the stone fights up and down the Pass, the wrestling matches and the demonstrations of how to fall gracefully (one of which went wrong when he damaged a leg at Dovestones Quarry). It took most of the day to make a suitable stew in a baby's bath we had found, and initially Slim would not let me take part, being too young and small. After an intercession by Joe I was allowed under sufferance to take part with the others, and I repaid Joe's faith in me by winning the competition, eating several bowls of delicious stew.

Having reached the age of eighteen, I had to register for national service. I could have been deferred, but the head of the printing college in Leeds advised I should get it over with and then return to studying. I had strong views about this and registered as a non-combatant, but was delighted when I was posted to the Army Pay Office on Manchester's Stockport Road. I lived in a civilian billet on Brynton Road, which led on to Dickenson Road where Joe lived at that time with his mother. My very first weekend there we all went pegging on High Tor, the weekend after to Stanage, the weekend after that to Wimberry and then up to Yellowslacks, followed by climbs further afield in Wales, the Lakes and Scotland.

Most of these trips were in the cold winter of 1954. I was used to roughing it with the Bradford Lads, but this was a different world of doss-ing: in caves, at the foot of crags, in broken-down shooting cabins. Joe seemed inured to the cold, and as I was by then his gentleman's gentleman, as long as he (actually his mother) provided good food to cook each week-end, I dared not complain, but I secretly planned as soon as I was able to buy a four-season sleeping bag. This was rather a wild dream, as I only received twenty-eight shillings pay each week from the army.

The Rock and Ice were the most 'together' of any climbing club at that time. Midweek, they would meet at Ron's parents' house on one night, the Palais at Levenshulme on another, and the YMCA in the centre of the city on the Thursday night to finalise the venue where they would meet up the following evening. They drank gallons of tea and talked climbing and climbers. I recall only Ray Greenall ever danced at the Palais. In between times, Joe persuaded me to go twice to see Audie Murphy in *Ride Clear of Diablo*: he was a real fan of Westerns and his reading was dominated by the 'Sudden' series of novels.

I nearly always used to arrive late at the club's venues, but nobody ever asked why. It was because I was a member of the Manchester Athletic Club and would first go to the Fallowfield track. When Joe returned from the successful ascent of Kangchenjunga in 1955, I ran into him in my running strip in Longsight as I headed home to change.

'What is a gentleman's gentleman doing running around like he's being chased by the police?'

'I have just met the greatest athlete in the world!' I confessed to him. 'Emil Zátopek. At the Olympic Games he won the 5,000 metres, 10,000 metres and the marathon. I doubt anyone will ever equal that.' But Joe remained unimpressed.

It was about this time that Archie retired through ill health. Joe asked me one day to give him a hand as he had now inherited the business. The task was to break up a large concrete floor, to do which he used brute force and a sledgehammer. I kept having a go with another sledgehammer, but after a few minutes I was kyboshed and relegated to tea boy. This made me think: I could run many miles without tiring, but Joe's fitness was of another kind. Watching him with a sledgehammer, I realised he was super-fit; his work had given him an outstanding physique for climbing.

It was also about this time that certain members of the group acquired nicknames. Joe became 'The Baron'. Ray Greenall became 'Anderl the Brew' because he looked a bit like Anderl Heckmair and could make a brew whatever the conditions! Whillans became 'The Villain'. The most inspired I think was 'Mortimer'. Joe Brown and Joe Smith had been climbing on High Tor, made illegal by the local council in the early 1950s for some unclear reason. Waiting for them at the top as they finished was the police.

'What are your names?' asked the copper in charge.

'Joe Brown and Joe Smith.'

'Can't you do better than that?' replied the constable.

It took quite some time before they established they were telling the truth, and they were then free to go with a caution. In order to avoid future confusion, with two Joes being one too many, Joe Smith became 'Mortimer', swiftly edited down to 'Morty'.

My two years in Manchester ended in 1956, but I stayed in touch with my friends there. In West Yorkshire, most of the Bradford Lads had moved away, taking advantage of the opening up of higher education. The only one remaining active in the region was the gentle giant John 'Ram' Ramsden. One weekend at Froggatt Edge, we met Peter Biven, then living in Leicester. He told of the magic land of Cornwall and its granite sea cliffs, of which Trevor Peck and he were pioneers. And so that summer, Ram and I decided to check this out. The ride down on his Royal Enfield Bullet motorbike was exciting. We climbed at Bosigran, Chair Ladder and Sennen. We saw no other climbers during the week we were there, although we did meet a very old A.W. Andrews who could justly claim to be the original Cornwall sea cliff pioneer. I reported all this to my Rock and Ice friends, and in 1957 a large number of the membership also decided to holiday in the South West, although Whillans, who was off to the Himalaya, chided us by saying we should wait to visit such places until we were old and past it!

In 1957, Joe married Valerie Gray, a teacher and climber from Blackburn. Slim was Joe's best man. As part of this change of status they joined the Cornish Riviera team. By that time, they were travelling in an Austin A35 van, while I and my passengers drove an Austin A40. They had a hunting horn and we had a bugle, and as we passed each other we would give a blast on these instruments. To see the Rock and Ice at the seaside was a revelation. We had a dinghy from which Joe exhibited his enthusiasm for fishing. We had heard that off the coast was a basking shark and we set out to catch it. We spent several hours at sea, all were sick and we never caught the shark. We did do a lot of climbing on the sea cliffs and all returned with happy memories of cream teas and the superb granite of the South West.

In 1958, a visit to the Alps was not to be denied. The best laid plans can pose a problem, however. Joe, Morty and I had been climbing on Clogwyn y Grochan. Joe challenged us to a race back to the tents after we had finished for the day. The descent from the crag was short but steep and we were going hell for leather when Brown took a screamer. Turning back, I saw him laid out in agony on the scree. Morty and I scrambled back up and pulled him back up to his feet, only to find he could not move unaided. We helped him down to the tents and he decided he must go to hospital. But there was a problem: neither Val nor Joe would countenance going to Bangor accident and emergency, as it had a bad reputation among climbers at that time. So we laid Joe full length in the back of my van and Val followed driving their A35, Morty directing me to Withington Hospital, Manchester, where we discovered Joe had fractured his leg. I do not know why he seemed to have a blind spot about running; he even had the confidence one weekend to challenge Eric Beard, one of the greatest fell-runners of his or any era, to a race up Cat Bells in Borrowdale. Beardie gave him a head start of half the fell but still beat him to the summit.

Joe made a quick recovery despite him limping badly on occasion and our plans for the Alps were still on. Val, Joe, Morty and I drove the A35 to the coast and left the vehicle there, catching the ferry and then trains to Chamonix. Whillans was already there when we arrived, recovering from an epic ascent of the *Bonatti* on the south-west pillar of the Dru. For our first climb, Joe decided that we – Joe, Morty and I – would ascend the north face of the Charmoz, but though we made ready to start out, the weather turned against us.

Back in the woods of the Biolay campsite, I was sharing a tent with Joe, Val having gone off on a journey with some French friends. All around us were British climbers, including some other Rock and Ice members. We were our usual messy crowd, and one day were embarrassed to be visited by some of the Chamonix guides, Lionel Terray among them, who were immaculately dressed. They had come to pay their respects to Joe Brown, leader of the Fissure Brown on his new route on the west face of the Blaitière in 1954, the hardest free pitch in the Western Alps. I was exercised in the use of my schoolboy French to translate.

Don, having recovered, joined Joe and Morty for an ascent of the west face of the Petites Jorasses. Feeling ill, I backed off the route. Down in Chamonix, I met Eric Beard, who had hitched there by himself, and went back to the woodcutters' hut, the famous Chalet Austria, which we made our base. He seconded me on an ascent of the *Ménégaux* route on the Aiguille de l'M. We then met Whillans, Morty and Brown and arranged that I would climb the east face of the Capucin with Don, while Morty and Joe would attempt the Dru by the *Bonatti*. The weather intervened, and although Whillans and I succeeded, we ended with a forced bivouac on our descent, while Joe and Morty had a less successful outing on the Dru.

While we were in Chamonix, we read in the media of how the Rock and Ice was to be disbanded. According to what we read, those who were currently the club's officers could not find others willing to occupy these positions. Whillans was furious at this news; Joe was his usual sanguine self. I had never formally joined, just attended. But the club's demise marked seven years of achievement, and a few years later, when I was living in Derby, Nat Allen and I reformed the club.

On the train home was in fact the only time I ever saw Joe lose it. There were no seats available and so we were sitting in the corridor on our gear. A ticket inspector came down the train and Joe stood up to show Val's and his ticket, at which the official called him a swear word, grabbed his gear and threw it as far as he could. The next we knew, Brown had grabbed him and pushed him up against a compartment door. The day was saved by Val, who spoke excellent French and explained we were *des alpinistes* on our way home from the Mont Blanc range, which was why we had so much equipment with us. We were not the idle dossers the inspector had believed us to be.

In 1959, Joe had his first taste of a professional film assignment, taking on the role of climbing stand-in for the lead actor in *Hazard*, a steel-industry safety film being shot in the Dolomites. He was accompanied by Don Roscoe, and the director was Tom Stobart, who had made the successful 1953 Everest film. I received a message that if I managed to get out to the Dolomites I too could find work on the production. I decided I had gone as far as I could working for a printer and publisher in Leeds, and so I recruited Eric Beard, Brian Fuller and Eric Metcalf to travel out with me in my van to share the cost. We met the filming crew in Cortina, where we spent over a month working on the film. It was truly an educative experience, mainly about how slow the filming process really is. It seemed that a few minutes of shooting took many hours of preparation. None of the 'stars' were climbers, but Joe was in his element, doubling as the hero, the beginning of his successful film and television work.

In 1960, I was administering a special unit: fine-art printing by photogravure for one of the biggest printers in the UK, who had five factories around the country. The unit was based in Derby. One day in the spring, Joe contacted me to ask if I would like to accompany him on a trip back to the Dolomites and Chamonix. Yes, I would, but the longest I could be away would be three weeks, which seemed ideal to Joe and our driver, Claude Davies, who was happy to go along for the ride. There was, however, a snag: Joe had developed a stomach ulcer (too many bacon butties), and so for the early part of our stay in the Dolomites we lived on Ovaltine and milk. So, the mantra was: start climbing late and finish early. Nevertheless, we climbed half a dozen routes, including the *Spigolo Giallo*, the north face of the Cima Grande and the *Pilastro di Rozes* of the Tofana, but had a rather gruesome time on the Civetta. We had not then started wearing crash helmets, and on the north-west face we were quite a way up when there was some stonefall, a piece of which hit Joe on his head as he was leading. He was wearing his flat cap, which offered no real protection, but for some reason he just kept on climbing and must have run out at least 300 feet of rope. When I finally joined him, his face was covered in blood. The last sections of the climb seemed harder than we expected, but I think it was the conditions rather than the climb that were so.

As we set out for the Western Alps, I had the only disagreement I ever had with Brown: I suggested we went via the Eiger's north face, but he made it plain he was not interested, and that he did not think that it was worth wasting our time on such a diversion. Arriving in Chamonix, we were met with the news that it was the worst season ever and that the snow level was down below Montenvers. We met up with Robin Smith and Dougal Haston and agreed that at the first break in weather we would try the unclimbed south face of the Fou.

There was finally an improvement in the weather, and the four of us set out for the Envers des Aiguilles hut the very next day. Just to reach the refuge was a challenging climb in itself, the slabs leading up to it being covered in ice and snow and requiring an axe and crampons. I would have liked a rope but dare not ask this company for one. Robin burned us off, for he started to sing, to illustrate he had plenty of puff left. We were the first climbers at the hut for days and were away before light the next morning. The way to reach the south face is via a couloir. We cowered on its left side as soon as we entered this, as first rocks and then snow whistled down.

'I'm going down,' I decided. 'This is suicide.' And as it was now getting light, that's exactly what I did. Before I'd reached the hut it had started to hail, then snow. I was just snuggled down in a pile of blankets when the others came clattering back to join me. Retreating to Montenvers that day we were in a mood of high spirits, jollity and grip. Back at the Biolay campsite we packed up and set out, with Claude driving us home in style.

Joe stopped being a property repairer in 1961 and became an outdoor pursuits instructor. He and Val moved to live in a flat at the White Hall centre in Derbyshire, during which time he became keen on canoeing. For some reason, he contacted me to make a canoeing trip with him, down the River Derwent. I was an absolute duffer at this, but agreed. All went well till we hit some faster-flowing water. Brown, who by then saw himself as an expert, ran flat out into a bridge support and I felt the resultant 'bang'. I followed on as carefully as I could and avoided the obstacle. When we finished, Joe had trouble getting out of his canoe; he had hurt his back in the collision. I phoned the next day to see if he was all right, but Val answered. Joe had gone to hospital and the medics had to pass him through a window as he could not get through their doorway, so stiffened up had his body become after reaching home. Typically, though, he was soon out and about again.

Val and Joe moved to Llanberis in 1966 to open the Joe Brown Shop in its main street. One of the more lurid of the tabloids ran this headline, 'The Human Fly moves to Wales,' so I sent a card addressed only to the *Human Fly, Llanberis*, and it reached him! In April 1966, the BBC made their famous live broadcast of Joe and an all-star cast climbing *Red Wall* at Gogarth, so amusingly caricatured by Tom Patey in his article 'The Greatest Show on Earth'. Joe was one of the stars, while I was a porter and part of the rigging team.

In 1967, for the *Vector* climb which was an ITV *World of Sport* production, once again Brown showed his media calmness when under pressure. I was in charge of recruiting the team of climbers who made this possible and was responsible for the camera operators' security. One memento I have of this is Joe singing his party piece 'The Sergeant Major' at the post-event party, recorded by the event's producer, Ned Kelly.

After the *Vector* climb, Joe and I went our separate ways. We remained close friends, and I visited him a few days before he died. We both agreed we had been so lucky to have lived the lives we had, beginning to climb in the late 1940s.

Joe was the outstanding climber of my generation and his record speaks for itself: over 600 new routes in the UK, and first ascents abroad including in the Himalaya, such as Kangchenjunga, the Mustagh Tower and the Trango Tower. At the age of sixty, he was still able to lead *Suicide Wall* again and to join an expedition to Cho Oyu. Nobody I know remained active for so long. But above all this, he was good company. When I was with him, we laughed a lot, except when we had to be serious. Fame never really meant much to him, and he remained the same person as when I first met him as a fifteen-year-old in the Wall End barn.

This article first appeared in the 2022 *Alpine Journal*.

5

THE VILLAIN: DON WHILLANS

'A diamond with a flaw is better than a common stone that is perfect.'

— CHINESE PROVERB

R ecently, a film-maker contacted me. They were planning to make a feature film about the life of Don Whillans, and he questioned me about the project: what did I think about it? I advised: 'If it is to be honest and truthful, it would probably need to be certified at the highest age level.'

'The Villain' was not a soubriquet that was applied to Whillans inaccurately. I studied psychology, and I know of happenings that would have earned him the 'sociopath' label. On occasion, his aggression was frightening to behold, but let us be clear: he was without doubt one of the outstanding mountaineers and rock climbers of any era.

It is in retrospect a surprising fact that he and Joe Brown emerged and were active together, starting to climb within a few years of one another. When the editor of one of the continental climbing magazines contacted me and asked to know who I thought were the three British climbers who I believed were the most memorable in the history of our sport, I had to admit that Whillans was one of them.

Don Whillans. © Leo Dickinson

I first met him in 1951 when I was fifteen years old and he was seventeen. I was jogging down the Llanberis track, having just made my first climb on Clogwyn Du'r Arddu with Jack Bloor, and he was coming the other way. I was carrying all our equipment and spare clothes since Jack had gone off on a training spin. (He was an outstanding runner, having won the Three Peaks Race in Yorkshire.) As I drew level with Whillans, he spat out an 'Ah doo'. He was only as big as I was then, five-foot-three, but he was twice as broad in the shoulders and he had the angular face and quiff in his hair which were to become such features of photographs of him in the media. I had not understood his greeting. He spat out another 'Ah doo'. He looked so aggressive that I stammered out a 'Hullo' and scuttled off down the track, followed by a shout of, 'Bloody stuck up!'

I next met him on a Rock and Ice bus trip to Glen Coe the following Easter, when I was his seat companion. He did not let me forget how I had reacted on our first meeting. I was subjected to a flow of acerbic comment the like of which I had not then experienced.

Don had a language that was all his own and finessed over the years. If you were easily put off, you were a 'drink of water'; if you confessed to finding a route hard, you were a 'ta ta'; if you advised him a climb was not in good condition, you were a 'ninnie'. But the biggest put-down was if you were a 'little hill man'. This might, on occasion – besides being accorded to a single subject – be meant for all and sundry in the climbing world whom he might be annoyed at.

The climbing partnership he enjoyed with Brown began in the spring of 1951. Don was paying his first visit to the Roaches in Staffordshire, and he wandered by accident into a first ascent scene on the Lower Tier. Joe had led up a crack which was repelling his second, and at his failure Whillans volunteered to try. He tied on and without too much difficulty reached the ledge on which the leader was belayed. He then expressed a wish to try the next pitch. Joe agreed to him trying, and with a struggle he succeeded. The route was called *Matinee* because a crowd had gathered to watch the action, and Brown was impressed that this youngster, who had only been climbing a matter of months, could lead what was near the top standard of that period, a pitch which was then also badly protected. It should be noted that it was generally believed at the time that one had to work through the grades, building up one's experience, before attempting extreme climbs. Whillans, like Brown, was a contradiction to such a belief: they were both able to ascend difficult routes after only a short novitiate.

Matinee saw the beginning of a partnership that lasted for several years, one of the strongest in the history of British climbing. The media loved these two working-class heroes: they fitted the belief that society was changing and becoming more egalitarian. Brown became known as the 'Human Fly', and in a Stockport paper, 'Whillans moved up holdless slabs balancing like a fairy'. He let it be known that if the journalist referred to him as such again, 'he would deal with him', but in later years he was happy to be referred to as the 'Andy Capp of the climbing world'.

I kept in touch with the Rock and Ice after the bus trip to Glen Coe, particularly with Ron Moseley. He sent me details of routes Whillans had pioneered on limestone at Stoney Middleton and on Dovedale's Pickering Tor in the Peak District. In the spring of 1953, John Ramsden and I travelled by train, bus and on foot to Stoney, where I led *Frisco Bay* and repeated some other routes Don had pioneered, but we had no other names and even pioneered a route of our own, *Little Capucin*. How we then travelled to Dovedale I do not now recall, but both Ram and I, despite many attempts, failed on Whillans's route across the roof of the cave at Pickering Tor. On Ron's advice we slept in some barns which the Rock and Ice secretary had recommended. One must realise that climbing on limestone was then not seen as the norm: it was mainly ascended by artificial means, as in the case of the main overhang at Kilnsey Crag, Yorkshire, by Ron Moseley and John 'Fritz' Sumner.

When I was posted to Manchester for national service in February 1954, I climbed mainly with Joe, Ron Moseley, Ray Greenall, Joe Smith and other members of the Rock and Ice Club, but with Whillans not so often. My memory of him at that time was that he worked on Saturday mornings and thus much of his activity was confined to outcrops that he could reach after his work had finished for the day. He was a plumber and proud of the fact. I remember how he reacted when Joe was also referred to as a plumber in a media profile. 'Nat Allen and I are plumbers,' he spat out. 'Joe is a bleeding property repairer,' which to his thinking was evidently inferior.

I did visit Cratcliffe and Froggatt Edge with him, and was stunned when after a route on the Pinnacle at the latter, he simply jumped off the top across the gap to the hillside opposite. Until a motorcycle accident in 1961, when he badly injured a kneecap, he was impressive at leaping and jumping. I was once at Curbar Edge with him, and I was leading Eric Beard up *Short Slab* when Whillans soloed up behind wearing boots. Beardie found the route hard, and was telling Don so as they arrived together. 'You can easily jump down this route,' Don advised, and without hesitating he turned round and ran back down the slab.

I asked him once why he had not done national service. 'Because I failed the medical,' was all he would answer, which I found unbelievable. I thought him physically an outstanding figure at that time, and as I was mixing with some of the best athletes in the country – one from our Manchester Athletic Club had just managed a four-minute mile – I thought his answer was a joke. But I was to subsequently find out that Whillans did suffer from a rare kind of vertigo which had previously hospitalised him, and that was why he had failed his medical.

Another fact which may surprise the reader was that in these early years, Don neither smoked nor drank much alcohol: he preferred to stay in the barn or his tent and listen to a small cassette radio while other members of the club visited the pub.

Don was fortunate that there were climbers in the Rock and Ice who had Alpine experience: in 1952 he joined Don Cowan and Nat Allen to visit Chamonix, and under their tutelage he learned the basics of how to become an alpinist. On a visit time-limited by work commitments, they managed three classic routes on the Aiguilles, including the Mer de Glace face of the Grépon. From such beginnings was his motivation born.

When the Alpine Climbing Group was formed in the spring of 1953,

Whillans, along with Cowan and Allen, were invited to be founding members. Later, I became its secretary, and Don was one of its keenest supporters, but when it was formed Joe had not even visited the Alps. This was to change in the summer of 1953, when Cowan, Allen, Don and Joe visited the Alps together. After an epic on the Crocodile, they did successfully climb the route, but on the descent a series of accidents led to a cut rope, with Joe in his crampons falling on to Whillans who received a punctured backside, and Cowan burning his hands holding the fall. They retreated to the Biolay campsite to lick their wounds.

Joe, looking through the guidebook, found that the Fissure Fix on the west face of the Blaitière was the hardest pitch in the range. They met up with Geoff Sutton and Bob Downes, two members of the Cambridge University Mountaineering Club; at that time, Sutton had probably the best knowledge of the Aiguilles of any British climber and he informed them that a huge rockfall meant that the route on the Blaitière was no more and was ripe as a new route. They set off to this at the first opportunity, Brown climbing with Cowan and Whillans with Sutton. It was on this first attempt that Joe led the Fissure Brown, a crack which came to be acknowledged as the hardest pitch in the Western Alps. Joe reported it was no harder than some of the gritstone cracks he had already ascended, but I am not so certain of that. Their first ascent of the face was stopped by the weather after a bivouac on ledges higher up.

They were back in Chamonix the following year, and after an abortive attempt on the east face of the Capucin, held up by the weather and a slow party ahead of them, Brown and Whillans wrote their name large in the history of alpinism with the third ascent – and the fastest – of the west face of the Petit Dru, and by completing their first ascent of the west face of the Blaitière. Near its summit, Whillans led a crack, the second crux of the climb, which he overcame by a fierce layback.

Whillans saw these successes as the way forward for him to become a full-time climbing bum. There was no doubt that with longer periods in the Alps many routes would be within his compass, and over the following decade the number of ascents he made marks him out as the leading British alpinist.

He was still pioneering in Britain, and though at times he was difficult to be with socially, once on a climb or an outcrop one could not wish for a more concerned companion. I climbed a lot with him in the late 1950s.

I was with him when he led the first ascent of *Cave Wall* on Froggatt Edge, and I made the second ascent of his Burbage crack climb *Goliath*. He wanted me to tell him if I thought this was a hard route, and worth recording. It is one of the hardest crack climbs of its era.

He coached me up the *Left Eliminate* on Curbar after I had to be rescued when my right boot became immovably stuck in the narrowing crack. I had a blank on this route, although I had already led *Peapod* and the *Right Eliminate*. He soloed it to show me how it was done, and he talked me up it after him.

I also climbed with him in the Mont Blanc range and the Dolomites. The hardest route I did with him was the east face of the Grand Capucin, and although we had no difficulty on the ascent, the descent, with a forced bivouac in a storm, tested us completely.

An interesting meeting occurred after that summer's Alpine season when we had a Rock and Ice meet at my parents' home in Woodhouse, Leeds. We climbed at Ilkley, Crookrise and Almscliff, and my father and Whillans started a surprising friendship which lasted until my father's death. My father was involved in the entertainment industry almost all his life, and Don accompanied him on some of his club and theatre dates around the north of the country. It was noticeable from this time on that Don became more ready with the apposite one-liners for which he became famous in the climbing world.

Don's first visit to the Himalaya was in 1957, when he was a member of the Masherbrum expedition. In retrospect, this had a real effect on his future physical well-being, for while travelling to Pakistan by sea, which took several weeks, he started drinking and smoking. Beer was a shilling a pint and he won a raffle prize of 1,000 cigarettes; by the time he had smoked them, he was hooked. I know from personal experience how hedonistic such sailings can be, having also travelled by such means on two occasions. There is little to do on these journeys except eat, drink and make merry. The attempts on Masherbrum were unfortunately held up when Bob Downes was taken ill with altitude sickness; sadly, he did not recover. This had a great effect on Don, for he had become close friends with Bob, and together they had pioneered *Centurion* on Ben Nevis. Despite a last attempt with Joe Walmsley backing him up, Whillans had to admit defeat despite being close to the summit of the mountain.

From then on, the Himalaya held him in thrall. He took part in the

Trivor expedition of 1960 and at its end drove back to Lancashire on his motorbike. He was also on the Gauri Sankar attempt in 1964, which I organised. I could extend this article by thousands of words, because this expedition was full of incident: we drove from Leeds to Kathmandu and were almost successful. I think Whillans's outstanding ascents in the 1960s were his two climbs in Patagonia: in 1962, the Aguja Poincenot with Frank Cochrane on an Irish expedition, and in 1963 the Central Tower of Paine with Chris Bonington.

Don's character when compared to Joe's was as different as chalk and cheese. Brown was calm and sanguine; Whillans in a temper was frightening. He never threatened me, but I saw enough of him out of control when riled to know not to get involved. On one occasion, Morty decided to challenge Joe to a wrestle-cum-fight, but included me in his plans. Initially, I refused, but Joe agreed, believing he could handle us both: growing up on the mean streets of Manchester he was used to dealing with heavies. Morty and I had a plan: he would take the Baron head on while I would creep up behind him and put a stranglehold on his neck. This worked a treat, and we nearly killed him. I was so sorry to have taken part, but when he recovered Joe was full of admiration. 'You clever little bleeders,' he observed. But then I realised that Whillans was making ready to join in, and then he came at us! I turned round and began to run away. He came after me. Fortunately, I kept running and he could not catch me, but as I went off up the Llanberis Pass road, he shouted after me, 'You are a bloody slippery Jim!', and that is what he called me from then on.

I saw him in several confrontations over the years, but none as frightening as the night he picked a fight with some members of the Sheffield chapter of the Hells Angels. This occurred one winter's night in the Little John pub in Hathersage. They were annoying him as he was seated near the door and every time one of them came through, having been to the bar, he felt a cold draught. But I was amazed when, as one of them came through carrying a tray of drinks, Whillans stood up and hit him with the swinging door. The Angel went down. Whillans swung round, grabbed a bar stool and herded the Angels away, while Audrey, his wife, Morty and I ran outside to my van. The engine revved up, and as we pulled away, Don came running and dived into the back.

Unlike Brown, Whillans was a sports player. At school, he took part in gymnastics, boxing and rugby. He was really keen on participating in the games sessions of the Rock and Ice, and when we played barn rugby, he played no holds barred. A particularly bloody session occurred in the Wasdale barn in 1960, when the young Doug Scott and Dez Hadlum also took part. Besides being climbers, both played for rugby clubs in Nottingham. I used to make sure I was on Don's team. However, Don was not the strongest physically among the club members: Morty was usually so – he could do one-arm pull-ups with either arm.

Whillans's other big interest at this time was darts, but despite cheating – he used to fiddle his score – he could never beat Eric Beard, who was once in a competition for the best players in the country: a youth spent in Leeds 6 and its run-down back-to-backs has its compensations!

When I lived in Derby, Nat Allen, his wife Tinsel and I visited Audrey and Don at their cottage in Crawshawbooth, Lancashire. Whillans had been sent there during the war as an evacuee, and he had happy memories of the area. Though the accommodation was spartan, Audrey was almost saint-like: how she put up with Don and his tempestuous character I never understood, but her welcoming could not have been warmer. She had married him in 1958 after a long courtship, so she must have known all too well what their life together would be like.

Crawshawbooth is not too far from the Bridestones grit outcrop – known to locals as the Kebs. Whillans had pioneered many boulder problems there. I managed the *Duck*, which made me quack, and the *Whillans Jam*, but I failed hopelessly on *The Villain*! Don was offering to buy a pint for anybody who could repeat it, which was impressive because he was a notorious tightwad, but it was to be a few years before he had to pay up. My keenest memory of this visit was waking up with their cat licking my face as I lay in my sleeping bag on the floor of the cottage.

Around this time, Whillans was trying to make a living as a freelance lecturer, and then later as an equipment designer. I suppose in both cases he was eventually successful, for his lectures were hardcore and humorous and really appealed to the climbing fraternity. Some of his equipment designs – a rucksack, the world's first sit harness and his 'box' to replace a tent on expeditions – were a success; others, such as the 'whammer', not so. We had one of the first designs of the 'box' on Gauri Sankar in 1964 and it weighed over seventy pounds. Carrying it up, climbing the 'Little Eiger' and traversing the north face to put it into an ice cave we had dug completely banjaxed me. Later, Don was to act as consultant to a specialist clothing firm which was trying to develop a range of outdoor clothing. This was aimed at the general market and especially the golfing and motoring fraternity. For a while, Whillans was to be found at the Open or Silverstone, but I'm afraid the jackets, although the design looked attractive, enjoyed only limited success.

When I arrived in Liverpool by sea in January 1965 from the Gauri Sankar expedition, Whillans and Terry Burnell were onshore to greet me; they had come for their personal gear from the expedition.

'You picked a good one there,' observed Don. 'What's next?'

'The south face of Annapurna I.' I laughed and showed him a picture of the face I had obtained from Jimmy Roberts before I had left Kathmandu. I had also discussed this objective with Mr Rana, the foreign minister of Nepal; he had promised they would give us permission to attempt it. We started to plan for this objective, but the Patterson incident occurred, causing Nepal to be closed to expeditions for the next few years.

In early 1969, Chris Bonington contacted me as Nepal had opened again and Nick Estcourt, Martin Boysen and he were keen to try Menlungtse. Did I think they would get permission for this? 'No,' I replied, but added that the South Face of Annapurna I was a possibility. I sent Chris the photograph of the face. I had just married and there was no way I could participate, especially in the organisation. I was more than pleased when Don and Dougal Haston were successful on this climb in 1970, but so sad at the death on the expedition of Ian Clough, one of our Gauri Sankar party and one of my oldest friends. It was also on this Annapurna expedition that Whillans saw a yeti – at least he did see some kind of animal, and the Sherpas who were with him were convinced it was one!

Subsequently, Don was a member of the 1971 International Expedition to Everest's South West Face, organised by Norman Dyhrenfurth, and the 1972 European expedition, led by Karl Herrligkoffer, to the same objective. On both, Whillans performed well and reached some of the highest altitudes then attained on this route, but both attempts were rife with dissension and argument. Although the expeditions were replete with stars of the climbing world at that time, they did not gel well.

I think that these three expeditions were the apogee of Whillans's Himalayan fame and career, but as is the wont of today's media, it was only fairly short-lived. It did lead to Don appearing on a live television episode of *This Is Your Life*.

In 1973, I persuaded Whillans to accompany me to visit the Leeds university climbing wall, then the most famous such facility in the country. In retrospect, compared to how walls have developed over recent years, it was very basic, but it was probably the first wall to illustrate what could be achieved by an improved level of fitness specific to rock climbing. Whillans, however, was unimpressed and could not be persuaded to try any of the problems I attempted to show him. We retreated to the Fenton pub nearby. 'There is no bloody adventure on climbing walls,' he decided, holding forth over the pints. I wonder what he would say today, now that there are hundreds of walls in the UK and that most newcomers to the sport begin their careers climbing indoors in such centres.

When I was at the BMC, I involved Don several times in accompanying me to national events to which we were invited. One was a reception at the Manor House in London and the guest of honour was the Duke of Edinburgh. He was working the crowd with an entourage of hangers-on and weaving his way round. Eventually, he arrived at Don and me. He knew vaguely who I was for I was a member of a committee he occasionally chaired. I addressed him: 'May I introduce Don Whillans, sir, one of our council's most famed members.' The Duke looked at Don and was a bit taken aback when Whillans, in his full Andy Capp rig, came out with his usual, 'Ah doo', and then held out his hand. The Duke's entourage looked on in obvious disapproval but had to be surprised when their charge grasped this offering and shook the Villain's hand in return.

Even more memorable was when he accompanied me to meet Margaret Thatcher at the House of Commons, when she was leader of the opposition. She wished to meet representatives of the national bodies of sport. I will not repeat the story of what happened on this occasion, for it is well known. Jim Donini, the American climber, was puzzled to learn from this that Whillans, an icon of the working class, was a keen supporter of such a right-wing figure. I have to observe from this that as soon as somebody like Don breaks their origin boundaries, they might, to paraphrase Shakespeare, 'ignore the means by which they did ascend'.

Towards the end of 1974, with the approval of the executive of the BMC, I put the names of both Joe and Don to the Honours committee for recognition of the great contribution they had made to this country's mountaineering. This seemed to be proceeding without a problem, until Whillans was involved in March 1975 in an outrageous incident that made the front pages of the national dailies. In the early hours after a drinking session in the Sportsman's, he was stopped on the way home by the police for driving erratically. This led to a physical confrontation: Don attacked the policeman, who called for backup. Five police eventually subdued, handcuffed and pushed him into the back seat of a panda, where two coppers sat on him. But not before he had lashed out with booted feet and damaged the panels of the car. When the case came before the Rawtenstall court, the only excuse that the defence could offer for Don's behaviour was that Audrey was ill at the time and was in hospital. In retrospect, he was lucky with his sentence: if it had happened today, he would have received a long period in custody. He was fined a considerable sum and banned from driving for two years.

While this was front page news, a lady phoned me from the Honours committee: 'Is this Mr Whillans who is appearing in the press for his misbehaviour, the person your council has put forward for an honour?'

'I am sorry, yes, he is.'

'Oh goodness, we cannot have such a person receiving an honour.'

When the honours were announced in that year's Birthday List, Joe received the MBE, but Don was omitted.

In 1976, Audrey and Don moved to Penmaenmawr in North Wales and opened a guesthouse. I visited them there and was surprised that Whillans had become keen on tropical fish; he had a large tank in one of the rooms. Over the years, he still went on many trips: to Yosemite, to Tirich Mir in the Hindu Kush, on a Doug Scott-organised trip to Shivling, to Patagonia again, to the jungles of Venezuela with a face climb of Roraima, and to Huandoy Sur in Peru with a Scottish party, before sailing down the Amazon with Dave Bathgate at the expedition's conclusion. He went to Alaska and was on Broad Peak in 1983 when Dr Pete Thexton tragically died of pulmonary oedema.

But his days as the lead climber on prestigious expeditions were at an end. Those who were involved in these were not willing to include him, for not everyone was willing to put up with his self-serving approach. He found solace in other activities: he and Audrey visited the Red Sea to try scuba diving, and he tried a parachute jump when he declared he fell like a meat safe. He spent much of his time visiting old friends: John Streetly in the West Indies, Ronnie Wathen in Spain. But the non-stop heavy drinking and smoking started to affect his health, and he began to look more in girth like a sumo wrestler than a mountaineer.

One of his last real climbs was an anniversary ascent for TV with Joe Brown of their outstanding route on Dinas Cromlech, *Cemetery Gates*. It was sad to watch how unfit he was and how he struggled, compared to Joe, his senior, who was still climbing well.

In my early days at the BMC, I was faced with two main problems, financial constraints, and somehow making the council more relevant to the mainstream climbing community. My proposal to achieve these ends was a National Mountaineering Conference. From the first in 1974, it was a success. And every two years, it was held at the Buxton Conference Centre. The major event of the gathering was the lecture on the Saturday evening, given by someone universally acknowledged as a 'name' in the climbing world. Over the years, the speakers included Kurt Diemberger, Cesare Maestri, Anderl Heckmair, Walter Bonatti and Peter Harding. In 1984, by general demand, it had to be Whillans. He certainly lived up to the occasion, and his lecture got off to a good start when a streaker ran across the stage, allowing Don to make one of his most famous one-liners: 'Well, I'll be buggered, and so will he if I can catch him!' A full house roared its appreciation.

On the Saturday lunchtime, we ran a cabaret at the conference and the main event on this occasion was the Miss Buxton competition. Half a dozen of us dressed in drag and, aping the Miss World competition, appeared before a group of women climbers chaired by Rosie Smith, deputy head of *Mountain* magazine. The competition was won by 'Donna' Whillans who, when asked, declared, 'My ambition when I grow up is to become a fat, hairy climber!' There was a serious reason for such apparent levity: it was to raise funds to purchase the Alex MacIntyre Memorial Hut at Onich; while the cabaret was underway, buckets were circulating round the Opera House and hundreds of pounds were raised.

During his final year, Whillans was back working as a plumber in the Manchester area. At the BMC offices we had a water leak in our toilets, so I phoned him and he came round. When he arrived on his motorbike, he had obviously been in some kind of confrontation, for his leather coat was torn and his face bloody.

'What on earth has happened to you?' I gasped.

'I was knocked off my bike by a car as I drove here.'

'Crikey, are you OK?'

'I got up off the road and chased after them and eventually overtook the car and stopped in front of it. They either had to stop or run me down!'

'Bloody hell, Don, it sounds like the Dukes of Hazzard.'

Whillans continued: 'The driver got out of the car and I flattened him, but none of the other three would get out and fight. They wound the windows up tight and I couldn't get at them. But I had my boots on, so I kicked the hell out of their car! Then I rode off.'

I was gobsmacked by this happening. Don was over fifty, and one would have thought he was past such escapades. I could only observe, 'Nothing has changed, has it Don?'

'You're bloody right, Slippery Jim.'

That summer he drove out to the Dolomites on his motorbike. He had been keen on this method of transport from his teenage years. He was supposed to meet Harry Smith but never made contact. At Alleghe, he did meet old friends Derek Walker and Roger Salisbury, but the latter noted how unfit and slow he was. Most of the time, he just sat around draped over a chair, sunbathing and drinking. On his drive home he ran into continuous heavy rain and stopped off in Oxford, wet and dispirited, at the house of an old friend, Derek Bromhall. After a welcoming meal and a few beers, he went off to bed but never woke up, having suffered a major heart attack. This was August 1985, and he was fifty-two.

Don's funeral was held a short while later at Bangor Crematorium. Despite everything, his death was mourned by hundreds of climbers from all over the country. I gave the oration and concluded that his was a unique character, difficult to assay but unforgettable.

After his death, we who were his friends felt there should be some kind of memorial to him. The original proposal was a campsite in Chamonix. Derek Walker and I met with local officials there, but the only offer we received for such a site had avalanche warnings for winter and spring use.

After discussions with Audrey, it was decided that a hut at one of the main climbing areas in the UK was what she would like to see. A committee was formed under the chairmanship of Derek Bromhall, and fundraising began. My effort in this was to organise a Don Whillans memorial evening at the Free Trade Hall in Manchester, where Doug Scott, Nat Allen, Joe Brown and Chris Bonington spoke of their climbs and memories of Don. Some friends of mine in Leeds owned a print workshop, and as they were climbers and wanted to help, they printed hundreds of leaflets for us, free of charge: *Buy a pint for Don!* Meanwhile, Derek and the other members of the committee fundraised a total of £50,000.

Fortunately, Rockhall cottage at the Roaches came up for sale – for over £100,000 – and this was purchased on a long lease with grants from the Sports Council and other bodies to make up the balance. This cottage, once refurbished, became the Don Whillans Memorial Hut, run by BMC volunteers. Truly appropriate, because it was here that Don met his one-time climbing partner Joe Brown and was where they made the first ascent of one of its most famous climbs, *Sloth*. And it was where Don met his future wife, Audrey, who opened the hut at a ceremony in 1993.

This article first appeared in the 2023 *Alpine Journal.*

6

BIG IN THE UK: ROYAL ROBBINS, JEFF LOWE AND WARREN HARDING

I cannot remember now how it came about, but in the latter part of the summer of 1965, Liz and Royal Robbins arrived in Leeds and stayed at my parents' house in Cookridge. By that time, we knew about Yosemite and its big wall climbs, the *Nose* route of El Capitan and the *Salathé Wall*. But in 1965, none of my friends had met any of the climbers involved in pioneering these epic routes, until Royal put in an appearance. When he did, it did not disappoint, for earlier that summer, partnered by John Harlin, he had climbed the *American Direttissima* on the Petit Dru.

Rumour had painted Royal as having a professorial demeanour, tall, spry, quiet and contemplative. This held good at the start of the Robbins's visit, as Royal took on my chess-playing friend and Almscliff guru Tom Morrell, sitting in my parents' living room while working out how to check-mate his opponent shortly after settling in.

The next day it had to be Almscliff, and as we toured the outcrop, I recounted the long history of the crag and its previous generations of pioneer climbers – Slingsby, Botterill, Frankland, Dolphin and so on. I realised what grabbed him most were the boulders. I had contacted Tony Barley about our guests' visit and with him in the lead we ascended the *Green Crack*, *Demon Wall* and the *Overhanging Groove*. I then led my party piece, *Great Western*, and Royal enthused that our climbs were 'intrinsic miniature masterpieces'.

Royal Robbins in 1966. © John Cleare

But Royal was not to be denied getting to grips with the boulders. Ascending such classic problems as *The Crucifix*, *The Niche*, *Fisher's Stride*, *Pothole Direct*, Royal was enjoying these. Then, near the Black Wall, he asked, 'Where are the no-hands problems?' Tony and I were stumped, as we had none of these in our playlist. And so our visitor began to work one of the classic slab problems nearby to show us how it was done, confessing that this was something he practised whenever possible. We quickly realised he was an expert at this, because after a few tries he could balance up and then descend the problem he had selected to illustrate this technique. Neither Tony nor I could match him and gave up trying after many failures. In fact, it took us some more visits and lots of attempts before we could emulate the American master.

Both Royal and Liz were easy to be with, for Liz was also a climber, and to hear from Royal first-hand about Yosemite and its climbs fired my imagination. I also learned about his early climbing career, starting out on the outcrops near Los Angeles and at Tahquitz. In 1952, as a seventeen-year-old, he had pioneered his first major new route on that cliff, the *Open Book*, a 5.9 climb and the first of that difficulty in the USA. Before visiting Yosemite, he had already spent two years as a participant on a rock climbing trip organised by the Scouts. He told me that he had gazed up at El Capitan and was informed by their course instructor that it would never be climbed.

Royal's breakthrough year was to be 1957 for, with Jerry Gallwas and Mike Sherrick, they pioneered the first ascent of the north-west face of Half Dome. This, along with Warren Harding's ascent of El Capitan by the *Nose* route the following year, ushered in the golden age of Yosemite climbing. For the next two decades, Robbins was one of the climbers at the forefront; the list of his first ascents is awe-inspiring.

To put this into some context, however, there were other climbers who are equally deserving of recognition. In 1961, Tom Frost and Chuck Pratt joined up with Royal – a team of equals – to make the first ascent of the *Salathé Wall* on El Capitan. Another key figure in the Yosemite revolution was Yvon Chouinard, who, along with Frost, Robbins and Pratt, pioneered the *North America Wall* of El Capitan in 1964. Chouinard was a key developer of the hardware that made some of the Yosemite climbs possible.

Unfortunately, just as I cannot now recall how Liz and Royal fetched up in Leeds, I cannot remember where we travelled to next except that we stopped off in the Peak District at Curbar Edge. I wanted to see how Robbins would deal with the *Right Eliminate*. This type of offwidth crack is meat and two veg to Yosemite climbers, and he did not disappoint, ascending it with some ease.

In 1966, when I was solo hitch-hiking from Mexico City to Yosemite, I carried with me an invitation to stop off at Royal's mother's home in Barstow, California. Which I did, and she fed me, washed my clothes and, as mothers do, recounted her son's early life battles, from a not-too-impressive school record, to how he had found his true self in the outdoors. Besides climbing, he had been a junior ski champion, attested to by the trophies on his mother's sideboard.

Over the next decade, Royal established himself as one of the most outstanding pioneers in the history of our sport: in 1967, he soloed the north face of Mount Edith Cavell in the Canadian Rockies; the following year, he made the first solo ascent of El Capitan via the second ascent of the *Muir Wall*; and in 1971 he made the second ascent of the *Dawn Wall* on El Capitan with Don Lauria. And he did so much more. Early in his climbing career he had been converted to boltless, pitonless clean climbing, using only nuts for protection. Along with Liz, he pioneered a demonstration route, the *Nutcracker*, to illustrate his ethics in Yosemite. 'Robbins exerted a moral leadership in both deeds as well as words,' observed Ken Wilson, editor of *Mountain* magazine.

In 1971, Royal published the first of his instructional books, *Basic Rockcraft,* followed in 1973 by *Advanced Rockcraft.* These were bestsellers, and in that era they were perhaps the finest expositions of where the sport was, technically.

Liz and Royal also founded a clothing store in Modesto called Mountain Paraphernalia, which morphed into the Royal Robbins clothing company. This was eventually bought out by investors, but which, despite the demise of one of its founders, is still trading strongly with Liz as a senior advisor.

Unfortunately, as the 1970s progressed, Royal was diagnosed with psoriatic arthritis which, as it developed, prevented him from serious climbing, so he took up adventure kayaking instead. Within a short period of starting this, he gained a reputation as an outstanding performer in that sport, making descents of some of the most challenging rivers in the Americas.

In 1992, Pat Ament wrote a biography of Robbins, according him the title, in spiritual terms, of *Spirit of the Age.* In his last years Royal also wrote a three-volume autobiography: *To Be Brave* was published in 2009; in 2010 came *Fail Falling,* and in 2012, *The Golden Years.* For some reviewers these were seen to be too matter-of-fact, too straight-laced, but they are an important historical record from someone who wrote honestly about his life and how it was to be a leader in the development of climbing during one of its most creative periods.

Royal died in March 2017. In an obituary published in the *New York Times*, John Branch described him as, 'the conscience of rock climbers'. I feel that more or less sums him up as the person I was lucky to have shared a rope with.

～

Jeff Lowe. © Jeff Lowe's Metanoia

In the winter of 1974–1975, I learned Jeff Lowe was paying a visit to climb in Scotland. Via friends, I managed to send him an invitation to travel to Manchester to give a public lecture before returning to the USA. I also suggested that if he had the time available, we could arrange a visit for him to do some outcrop climbing on gritstone. I think it was the latter which appealed, and by return I received a message from him agreeing to take this on. At that time, Jeff was already one of the most accomplished climbers in the USA, pioneering rock routes at the highest standards of the day but also by 1974 specialising in ice climbing: the pictures then circulating of his first ascent with Mike Weis of the Bridal Veil Falls at Telluride were truly inspiring.

Jeff eventually arrived in Manchester and his lecture enjoyed a full house and a rousing reception, after which I started out to drive him to my home in Yorkshire. All went well until we were nearly at our destination. Just as we started up the Hollins Hill out of Shipley, my terrible Russian car started to splutter, choked out and stopped: I had run out of petrol! And as to be expected in a 'grim up north' story, it was a terrible night of cold weather with driving rain. What to do, what to do? There were no garages nearby or open at midnight in those days. I explained to my passenger the problems we faced, but as a commentator was to write in tribute to Jeff at his demise, he was a 'pathological optimist'.

'How far is it to your house?' he enquired. 'Could we push the car there?'

'It will take about thirty minutes on foot,' I gasped out.

'OK, let's go!'

After kitting ourselves out, we set forth and walked to my home, by which time we were like wet rags. But Jeff never complained, and once arrived and sitting in our kitchen grasping a mug of tea, he laughed at my stories of the trials and tribulations of driving a Russian-made car.

Early next morning, Jeff and I retrieved my car and despite it being a very windy and cold day he still wanted to go climbing. At least it was not raining, but on arriving at Almscliff it was so wild I thought we could not snatch a route. Once again, however, his optimism was infectious, and after battling against the wind while tramping around the different faces of the outcrop, we found that down in the rift by *Square Chimney* and below the *Whisky Crack,* the wind was not so strong, so we roped up. I decided to ascend via the *Pigott's Stride* to reach the *Crack,* and when I explained the former had been pioneered by C.D. Frankland in the 1920s, Jeff was also keen to climb this. Looking at my partner, he was every Yorkshireman's idea of a US climber: tall, blond and athletic. I wondered if he would like to lead the *Whisky Crack* if I managed the *Stride.* To do this you first climb the sheer side of the Matterhorn Boulder then from near the top of that, bridge spectacularly across on to the main rock face. Having climbed this many times, I succeeded, despite the conditions, and then belayed below the *Crack.* Jeff, enjoying the gymnastics, came swarming up to me.

'Would you like to lead the *Crack*?'

'Sure, sure!' and up he went.

Pulling over the top, the wind was so strong it nearly blew him back down the face. Once I had joined Jeff, to get out of the gale we ran down and into the rift from where we had started. We then packed up and raced back to my car. A retreat to a cafe in Otley was followed by a trip to the Cow and Calf rocks above Ilkley, but the wind was even worse there. After some attempts at bouldering on the Calf, we headed back to my home in Guiseley to spend a pleasant evening dining and over a few brews talking about climbing and mutual friends. Jeff had heard of 'The Legend of Joe Brown' and I had to play and sing it for him.

The next day, he was heading south to London. I bade him goodbye at a drop-off at the Leeds railway station. I never saw Jeff again, but followed his subsequent incredible climbing career with keen interest. I use the word 'incredible' to describe Jeff's record of ascents over the next decades correctly: Will Gadd, no slouch himself, wrote about these as follows: 'There isn't one sector of climbing that Jeff hasn't excelled in or helped create.' I will highlight here just a few, for he made more than 1,000 first ascents, and to do that, you had to start young, which he did with his father Ralph and brothers Mike and Greg. With them, he climbed the Exum Ridge of the Grand Teton at seven years of age. By his teens he was pioneering 5.10 and 5.11 routes such as *Airtime* and *Pass or Flail* in Ogden Canyon, in the Wasatch mountains of Utah. Later, he visited Yosemite to make early ascents of the *Salathé Wall* (the seventh), *North America Wall* (the fifth) and the *Triple Direct*.

Born in 1950, he revelled as a young climber in his home state environment, tackling the high sandstone cliffs of Zion and southern Utah, his most famous route being the *Moonlight Buttress*. It was, however, in the high mountains that he made his most impressive ascents – in the Canadian Rockies, the European Alps and the Himalaya. In the latter, a solo new route on the south face of Ama Dablam in 1979; a solo of the south-east spur of Pumori in 1983; the north-west face of Kantega with Alison Hargreaves, Tom Frost and Mark Twight in 1986; and a solo attempt by a new route on the west face of Makalu in 1993. In 1990, climbing with Catherine Destivelle (and with David Breashears filming), he also made a repeat of the *Yugoslav Route* on the Nameless Tower of Trango in the Karakoram. His 1991 direct route on the north face of the Eiger, *Metanoia,* climbed solo in winter over nine days, was more than a standout climb. It was finally repeated in December 2016, after many failed attempts, by Thomas Huber, Roger Schaeli and Stephan Siegrist. A film was made in 2014 about this route and its history, *Jeff Lowe's Metanoia*, as by that date, tragedy had struck its pioneer.

There is so much more to the Jeff Lowe story: his equipment innovations such as Hummingbird ice tools, Foot Fangs and Snarg ice pitons, and his development of winter clothing, originally working with his brothers Greg and Mike at Lowe Alpine, then on his own at a new company he founded, Latok Mountain Gear. In the 1990s, he was responsible for developing 'mixed grade' climbing, with routes like *Octopussy* (M8): he introduced these 'M' grades for climbs that require both ice climbing and dry tooling.

In the same decade, he organised one of the earliest sport climbing competitions at Snowbird, Utah, and in 1996 he founded the Ouray Ice

Climbing Festival. He also produced three books about ice climbing, its history and techniques, of which *The Ice Experience* is a classic. He also produced three instructional videos on the subject. So far, the Jeff Lowe story is one of marvellous success, one of the most influential climbers ever, recognised as a leading proponent of alpine-style climbing; because of all this, he was made an honorary member of the Alpine Club and the American Alpine Club.

But then personal disaster struck in the early 2000s, for he developed coordination and balance problems, and fell victim to a neuro-degenerative process similar to motor neurone disease. This he faced bravely and somehow managed to keep in touch with a wide group of friends around the world at climbing festivals like Kendal and Ouray, despite being wheelchair bound, and by using social media. His death in August 2018 made many of us who had been lucky to have known him accept the example he exhibited throughout the long fight against his illness: to *carpe diem*, and fill every day with hours well spent.

❦

In 1980, at the BMC conference in Buxton, the celebrity lecture on Saturday – The Reflections of a Broken-Down Climber – was given by Warren Harding. I had tried to persuade him to do this for some years, for I had met him in 1966 in Yosemite and felt that he would, in theatrical speak, 'knock 'em dead'. His approach to climbing was in keeping with the British approach at that time. In the USA, he was known for his doggedness, drinking and farcing, as reflected in his motto *semper farcisimus*, which indicated his truly exuberant and iconoclastic character.

His lecture, thankfully, was well received. Afterwards, as with Jeff Lowe, I persuaded him to travel with me to my home in Guiseley, and to try some gritstone climbing. The following day I took him out to Caley Crags. After some easy soloing, I led him up the *Central Route,* a Very Severe on the Sugar Loaf Boulder and a local 5a classic. This made him think, and he stopped almost halfway at a delicate move to observe, 'You know, Dennis, I am going to need to do a lot more of this, or a lot less.' I realised his problem was a lack of reach, for he was short, squat and powerful, but this was a balance problem. If you are not used to gritstone climbing, it takes some time to realise how good in dry conditions the friction is. Warren put a foot high, rocked over and he was up and, in joining me, was laughing loudly at a new-found ability. For me to be climbing with the pioneer responsible for the most famous rock climb in the USA, the *Nose* route of El Capitan, was truly memorable. Yet talking with him, I realised that although he was a central figure in the development of multi-day big wall climbing in Yosemite, public recognition of this meant little to him.

Harding was born in 1924 and grew up in California, near to Lake Tahoe. After meeting a climber in the late 1940s who persuaded Warren to accompany him to make ascents of Mount Whitney, the Palisades and the Minarets in the Sierra Nevada, he started to climb seriously. It was, he observed, the first thing he had found that his brute stupidity made him successful at! He went on to pioneer twenty-eight first ascents in Yosemite, but the *Nose* of El Capitan in 1958 and the *Dawn Wall* in 1970 – then known as the *Wall of the Early Morning Light* – remain his most recognised.

Harding, unlike Robbins, was prepared to push his routes by any means he felt necessary, to do which he freely used pitons and bolts despite the strictures of those he dubbed the 'Valley Christians'. The *Nose* was an impressive feat of endurance. Partners came and went, sections were climbed, retreats followed. In all, Harding spent forty-five days on the route, but finally, accompanied by Wayne Merry, George Whitmore and Rich Calderwood, he was successful.

The *Dawn Wall* was different. Warren and Dean Caldwell spent twenty-seven nights on the wall. There was no yo-yoing, and Harding was given the appellation of 'Batso' in deference to his remarkable ability to live life on such vertical cliffs. To do this, he had developed specialised equipment such as the 'BAT' tent and the 'BAT' hook. Typical of Warren, when he was queried about his use of such naming, he explained that this acronym meant 'Basically Absurd Technology'. Noting how these climbs were achieved, a modern tyro might think spending so many days and nights on these routes is not impressive, but with the knowledge and equipment then available they were outstanding achievements.

In 1975, Warren was persuaded to write *Downward Bound,* which spelled out his rebellious and charismatic character. It contains anecdotes and stories from his ascents of the *Nose* and the *Dawn Wall*, but also farcical instruction in basic climbing techniques and humorous accounts of the climbing controversies and lifestyles in the 1960s and 1970s. I thought the title was a tilt at Outward Bound, but no: he chose that because it reflected the failure of his career as a responsible wage earner, due to his urge to go rock climbing.

Success for Harding in an establishment world was always just out of his reach, beginning with him being rejected by the draft board due to a heart murmur. After working through the Second World War as a propeller mechanic, he formally trained as a land surveyor. He held a union card all his life and worked on construction jobs in Vietnam and Alaska. On one such contract, he was hit by a truck which resulted in an injured leg and a limp for the rest of his life.

Warren loved to tell stories against himself. As I drove him to catch his flight back to the USA the day after we had climbed at Caley, he recounted how once in Yosemite he had teamed up with a visiting British climber who was short in temper. They managed to get their ropes in a tangle, and this became worse as Harding tried to untangle them.

The Brit exploded: 'My God, Harding, you cannot do anything right!'

Warren's response was classic: 'Yes I know, but I can do it forever.'

After the 1980s, he did little climbing, retiring to the northern hills of the Sierra Nevada, drinking cheap red wine and hot-air ballooning with friends. He died in 2002, but on the fiftieth anniversary of the *Nose* climb, the US House of Representatives passed a resolution honouring the achievement by Harding and his party. So, despite all, he finally was recognised by the establishment.

This article first appeared on *Footless Crow* in February 2019.

7

AN INTERVIEW WITH ALLAN AUSTIN

I conducted this interview for the *Leeds University Union Climbing Club Journal* of 1973, the editor of which was Bernard Newman. It is fair to say that at that time, Allan was a – *the?* – leading pioneer of Yorkshire and Lakeland climbing.

DENNIS GRAY: Do you have any fondness for such interviews? 'Allan Austin tells all!' Do you think they serve any useful purpose?

ALLAN AUSTIN: No, I don't think they serve any useful purpose whatsoever. They merely provide an easy way to collect a load of print for a magazine.

D.G. Much of my early climbing was undertaken with the now legendary Bradford Lads, who were at the forefront of British climbing in the late 1940s and early 1950s. I once made out a 'family tree' and was surprised at the links, some tenuous, but others close, between that group and most of the leading climbers who followed over the next decade. I believe your early climbing was done with one of the Lads, Mike Dixon?

A.A. No, I used to climb with Brian Evans and Mike was a friend of his. The first time I actually climbed was with Ashley Petts, and the next on a Mountaineering Association beginners' course in Llanberis. This was organised by Robin Collomb at Christmas 1955.

Allan Austin. © Dennis Gray Collection

D.G. You were very lucky in having Brian Evans as a partner in those early days. In my opinion he was one of the steadiest and most underrated climbers of his generation. When I first met you in 1956, I thought, *This guy will either win fame or end up lame!* Your climbing was characterised by strength, determination and drive, which often led you out of your depth!

A.A. There is a fair amount of truth in that! We used to climb as a team of three; we needed the third man to rescue the leader after he had run out of strength. We recruited Doug Verity, a big bloke who could stretch out his hands flat so I could stand with all my weight on them! I climbed with Brian because he was of my age group. I had transport and I was keen, and he was a good climber with no transport. Brian's idea was to climb at Very Severe. He was the only bloke in the club [the Yorkshire Mountaineering Club] besides Ashley who consistently led at that standard. They were not really hard, you know, but with the aid of my transport we had a lot more opportunities, and therefore we became very good as a result.

D.G. So initially you feel that Brian Evans was the driving force of your group?

A.A. Definitely. Brian would say, 'We'll do this route', or, 'We'll try up there.' The first big route we pioneered was *Stickle Grooves* on Pavey Ark. Brian had said to me in the club hut at Ilkley, 'We'll go to the Lakes and repeat Dolphin's climb, *Chequer Buttress*.' It had not then been repeated. And then once there, he noticed a big gap near to this, so we filled in this gap and also climbed *Chequer Buttress*.

D.G. In the late 1950s, you pioneered many outcrop climbs, but just like many others before and since, you used aid which has been shown to be superfluous. I am thinking of climbs at Brimham such as *Hatter's Groove* and the first pitch of *Minion's Way* where you stood on your second's shoulders!

A.A. No, I didn't. We had spent a month trying it like that, but in the end we climbed it free.

D.G. Well, that is as maybe, but today you are feared by young climbers who do make similar errors, for you will, and rightly so in my opinion, speak out against such mistakes. But is this not a case of 'the kettle calling the pot black?'

A.A. Everybody makes mistakes, and I think I have fewer pitons per foot climbed of any climber of my own time. Up to 1960, we had pioneered 200 or so new routes, and I don't think we used aid on any route on grit-stone, except for *Hatter's Groove*. In the Lake District, out of a hundred new climbs, only half a dozen pitons were used. I am not proud of using these, for I am weak like everyone else, but having said that I will stand back and realise that utilising them was a mistake. I for one do not try to back my 'blunders' up.

D.G. Having read the recently published *Fell and Rock New Climbs* booklet, I was surprised at the amount of aid the new generation of pioneers are allowing themselves to use in the Lake District. Do you think that some climbs are being forced today that should be left until standards rise further, in order that they can be climbed without such methods?

A.A. Oh, hell, aye! The prime example of this is *Peccadillo*. This had been tried by Geoff Oliver, Les Brown and several other outstanding leaders; they had all failed to solve this problem. But along comes a modern team, who also could not climb this route, and so they abseiled down and fixed an *in situ* sling, which they then used to get them over the difficult section. I reckon this sling marks the point at which they failed, and it has solved nothing. It was not a legitimate ascent, and it should not be recognised. Climbers now seem to be picking a line up a cliff and using just enough aid to make sure they are successful in climbing it, without really considering if the climb would be possible without this. I am not in a position any more to change things. Once, I might have climbed such routes without resorting to aid, but I cannot any more. Shouting is not enough; it really needs some very good climbers to be active in the Lake District again. An example needs to be set. If three or four of the area's leading climbers are using a lot of aid, then other people are bound to follow their example.

D.G. Don't you think in some of these cases a stronger line should be taken by the guidebook editors?

A.A. Yes, I do. In the new Langdale guide, I have been fairly courageous and have cut out three routes which had utilised excessive aid. If the artificial section of a climb is the main part, then we have not included it. For example, *The Pod* on Pavey Ark, ascended by John Barraclough using seven pitons for aid. It has subsequently been repeated using only two. In general, there is too much of a rush to climb a new route and then get it into print. This is a very bad thing for the sport.

D.G. Do you think the magazines are to blame for this?

A.A. In part; the system of first ascent lists at the back of a guidebook is also to blame. I much prefer Dolphin's system of a paragraph about each crag, picking out the historical highlights.

D.G. I can't say that I agree with you there. You mentioned Dolphin; you never knew him, but you have repeated many of his hardest climbs. In the early 1950s there was nonsense abroad about Joe Brown having created a 'new standard' in rock climbing, a 'breakthrough'. But I believe that Dolphin had already achieved this on outcrops, as had Peter Harding before Brown and Whillans.

A.A. You are right, but it was only for a short period. When Joe started pioneering his new routes in Wales, Dolphin's routes in the Lake District were of the same standard. But by 1953, Brown's routes such as *Surplomb* and *Black Cleft* were of a new grade, but not his earlier climbs such as *Cenotaph Corner* and *Hangover*, which were only as hard as routes like *Do Not* in Langdale.

D.G. Dolphin was improving every year though. For example, he had climbed a long way up *Delphinus* and examined many new possibilities on the East Buttress of Scafell before his death. But returning to your early career, you were among the first to try to prick the Rock and Ice bubble. I do remember your article, 'The White Rose on Gritstone'!

A.A. Ken Wilson, the editor of *Mountain* magazine, described it as one of the most biased articles he had ever read!

D.G. You were a little carried away in your attempt to break down the myths. I can remember you standing on Joe Brown's shoulders when you got into trouble on the *Deadbay Crack*! This attitude did tend to grind a little with us Rock and Ice members after witnessing such a performance.

A.A. Well, Joe Brown had pointed Mortimer Smith and myself at this climb and then sat back and watched while we failed on it. He had to rescue both of us from the crux, but I was the one who led it in the end. It took me four hours!

D.G. I led this climb a short while later and found it reasonable. Was it that you were psychologically bamboozled?

A.A. No, it was the fact that it was at the limit of my climbing ability at that time [1956]. The same day, Mortimer and I had failed on *Peapod*.

D.G. Do you accept, though, that some of your statements in that article were a little outrageous?

A.A. The article was written to be provocative. I decided years ago that if you were not opinionated in an article, then it was not worth reading, so I deliberately intended to annoy the reader. It seems I did not succeed in this, but I certainly did provoke some people! To be honest though, at that time there was no one to approach the Rock and Ice on gritstone. There were odd climbers, like Pete Biven, Pete Hassell and me, who were trying their easier routes, but the climbs that they considered hard, such as the *Right Eliminate*, we did not even look at. It took us a full year or more to catch up, and to develop the necessary techniques and standards. But in 1956, we were lucky if we managed to climb any of Joe Brown's or Don Whillans's routes!

D.G. It seems to me now, looking back over these years, that contemporary climbing historians have a wrong view of events in Wales towards the end of the 1950s. A recently published book has it that in North Wales in 1957, only one climber, not a member of the Rock and Ice Club, was climbing the hard, major Cloggy routes. I am sure you will recall Metcalf repeating some of these big climbs in 1956, and you yourself were making early repeats in 1957. Why do you think these reports are so inaccurate?

A.A. Because they were so parochial. I can remember John Disley telling me that when you had four climbers leading Very Severes in the Llanberis Pass, that they represented the climbing strength of Britain. This did not include people like Dolphin and his friends, active in the Lake District, or the Creagh Dhu in Scotland who were actually climbing at a much higher standard than Very Severe. He could not see past Harding, Moulam, Lawton and himself. This attitude ran on into the late 1950s when archivists like Rodney Wilson had prepared lists which included the first five or six ascents of routes like *Cenotaph Corner*. He'd never heard of Metcalf or Pete Greenwood! Rodney once informed me that I had done the second ascent of the *Black Wall*, but I already knew that John Ramsden had repeated it four years earlier.

D.G. Why do you think you have always concentrated on rock climbing? You have visited the Alps, but you now seem to confine your activities to West Yorkshire and the Lake District. Why is this?

A.A. My holidays have always been short, a fortnight at the most, and working on a Saturday morning meant that I had to get time off to travel to Wales. Hence, the nearer climbing areas were of necessity my goal. On one holiday I took in the Alps it rained and snowed for two weeks. I did not get up a single route! So, we travelled on to the Dolomites, where the weather there would also mean no climbing for several days. At one time, however, it did seem that we concentrated on and climbed only in the Lake District. But for a five-year period before that, we alternated weekends between there and Wales, and in fact I had managed all but two of the routes in Don Roscoe's guide to the Llanberis Pass.

D.G. You never managed many new routes in Wales, but you were always out in the front as a pioneer in the Lake District.

A.A. I thought that the Lake District needed a spur to bring it up to the standard of Welsh climbing, and so I was prepared to sacrifice myself for that cause. We only travelled down to Wales to attempt Joe Brown's routes. It seemed to me, then, that there were bigger and harder routes in Wales, and so we concentrated on the Lake District to try to develop the same there. At that date, 1959, there were ten Extreme climbs in Wales for every single one in the Lakes.

D.G. Did you manage to carry this policy out?

A.A. Yes, we pioneered some hard climbs but none as big as the famous Welsh routes. Unfortunately, we never found any Cloggys. All we discovered were climbs like those in the Llanberis Pass, so all the major classics in Wales are unmatched in the Lake District. There cannot be a dozen climbs in the Lakes which compare to the top sixty in Wales.

D.G. Can you still do one-arm pull-ups?

A.A. No. I could only ever do those at all on the door of the Ilkley hut, which was at such a height that I could start with my arm slightly bent.

D.G. In the last few years there has been a tremendous increase in the use of indoor climbing walls. I have visited the Leeds university wall in the past and last year I became a regular visitor, but this year it bores me. Perhaps it is because I cannot compete against the youths one now finds there, climbers like John Syrett, John Stainforth and that long-haired yob, Bernard Newman! The last time I saw you there, you were not exactly 'number one'. Do you mind being burned off by the younger generation, or will you keep on going until you draw your old-age pension?

A.A. No, I do not mind them burning me off. I go to the wall mainly for the social side, to meet other climbers: they are not such a bad lot, really. I went there once on my own and spent twenty minutes before going home because I was bored. It is the people who go there which make the wall an interesting venue, but it might be the competitive element as well.

D.G. Climbing in this country is very parochial. I think West Yorkshire climbers are as guilty of this as any, including the Scots! Why do you think these attitudes exist: Lakes versus Wales, Yorkshire versus Derbyshire?

A.A. It is just nationalism I suppose. Everyone likes to believe that they come from a special area. When I first started climbing, I did not care two hoots whether it was the Lakes or Wales, and that was true until I met Joe Brown. His remarks about Yorkshire and the Lakes tended to get my back up, and I guess it all stemmed from that.

D.G. Do you think that was a deliberate tactic on his part?

A.A. Oh, hell, aye! Joe has spent his life knocking others, he never stops doing this. One-upmanship is Joe's life.

D.G. Do you think this is because Brown has a superiority complex?

A.A. No, I think he just likes to set people up. It is his form of humour. He hasn't got a superiority complex and he is not an inverted snob like some of the other members of the Rock and Ice. A typical remark to me after I had failed on a route would be: 'I always said you were the best climber to come out of Yorkshire, but really they've never been much good, have they?'

D.G. Of all the routes which you have pioneered, which gave you the most pleasure and which do you think was the hardest to complete?

A.A. The *Wall of Horrors* gave me the most pleasure. It had been a long-standing problem and the scene of many previous attempts. Climbing a route with such a long history is always satisfying, even more so than discovering a new line. I had been trying it for a couple of years. Nowadays, one might resort to using aid, a peg or a sling, in case someone else came along and bagged it before you.

D.G. I remember Dolphin telling me, as a boy, of his top-roped ascent of the *Wall of Horrors*. And he had decided to leave it to be led on sight by the next generation. He sensed that there was a change in climbing ethics and considered that on-sight leads should be encouraged for first ascents. I was upset when you continually top-roped the route before leading it. I think it would have been better if you had led it on sight. Do you still think that you were justified in your methods when Dolphin had already shown it was feasible?

A.A. A top-rope ascent does not show that the route is possible, and anyway in that era most of the hardest gritstone routes had been top-rope inspected before their first ascent. I once saw John Gosling leading a new route at the Roaches in Staffordshire. He was able to clip into a piton, which had been pre-placed on an abseil rope, without even looking for it. He made the route look easy! I agree that sight leading is the most satisfying way to climb, but on outcrops where standards have always been pushed, I do not think that top-roping will ever be abandoned.

D.G. You have climbed at Harrison's Rocks in Kent. Do you think that the routes there should be led as a matter of course, instead of being top-roped?

A.A. Yes, climbing at Harrison's should employ the same techniques as any other outcrop, for example Almscliff. The rock is generally quite sound enough.

D.G. Several of your friends have been killed while climbing. Do you think that such a loss is worth the sacrifice?

A.A. Climbing is not worth getting killed for, but without some spur you just would not try. The reward in climbing is the intense personal satisfaction of having overcome a challenge with a certain level of danger involved. Without that danger there would be no point in going climbing – you might just as well be in a gymnasium or on a climbing wall! The only reason you go out on to a mountain is because it is such an unfriendly place, and you overcome the difficulties. Nowadays, we make up a lot of rules, put them into a straightjacket and call them climbs.

D.G. I have found that one of the best aspects of climbing is the friendships that you might make.

A.A. If you climb a lot, you meet other people who climb a lot and who have the same attitudes as you. Under stress, even if it is voluntarily induced, you find a lot out about people, and if what you discover is good, then they become a friend.

D.G. Do you reckon this is why women have not so far fitted into climbing circles, because they are not in a position to strike up these kinds of friendships?

A.A. Basically, I think women are motivated differently, for they have no need to try. Man's role has always in the past been the breadwinner, and up until recently women have never been in a competitive situation. I cannot think of another reason why women are not interested in climbing. They are only interested in the blokes, not even in the other women. The proportion of women who climb for climbing's sake is small.

D.G. What is your opinion of solo climbing? I refer to the sight of soloing hard routes, because your maxim has been, 'Sane men only lead on sight where there is some protection'.

A.A. I would like to be able to solo really hard routes. If it gives a climber a kick to solo a climb, then I have nothing against it, because we go to the mountains basically to enjoy ourselves.

D.G. Who do you think has been the most outstanding climber of your acquaintance?

A.A. The most impressive climbers I have ever climbed with were Joe Brown, Pat Walsh and Don Whillans. Of them all, I think Whillans impressed me the most. I could not understand how Joe climbed, but Whillans climbed like myself, only better. I do not know what made Walsh climb, but he also climbed better than me, although he did not have any sense of dedication as far as I could see. He did not seem to have any drive, his techniques were not marshalled, he just walked up to the foot of a rock face and ascended it. Whillans climbed just like I did: he thought about a route and arranged protection like I did, only better. Joe's style was completely different: he never climbed like anyone else I have ever seen. He had a style all of his own and I could not assess how he achieved this.

D.G. I think this was the basis of Joe's ability to psychologically bamboozle the people he climbed with. Moseley failed to follow him on the first ascent of the *Boulder*, which Ron himself was capable of leading quite easily.

A.A. True. Brown broke almost all the men he climbed with as regular partners. When you think of how good they were when they first started climbing with Joe, they were almost without exception climbing worse when he stopped climbing with them. The only climber who did not was Whillans. Presumably he was good at the beginning of their partnership, and he 'grew up' with Brown.

D.G. To switch to a lighter tone: the subject of climbing names has always fascinated me. It has been almost a social commentary on the development of our sport. I think you have been one of the climbers who has continually managed to produce excellent names. I am thinking of such names as the *Ragman's Trumpet* and *Man of Straw*. How do you keep coming up with names like that?

A.A. Well, generally I am told by other climbers that my names are poor. The people who climb with me generally title the routes; they do not accept my names.

D.G. So, someone else deserves all the credit?

A.A. *Ragman's Trumpet* was a particular line on Bowfell. The Tomlin team rolled up one day and they declared, 'We will climb that one day, by God, and we'll call it the Ragman's Trumpet!' They were getting at me, I suppose. *Man of Straw* was myself; I just did not like placing that peg. I have done the route since without it, and there is not much difference in standard.

D.G. Mass-circulation climbing magazines are here to stay, and their circulations continue to rise. In my opinion, you are no mean writer, and some of your articles over the years must be among the finest to appear in climbing journals. Why is it that you have never contributed to any of the mass-circulation climbing magazines?

A.A. The effect that these magazines have on climbing is a bad one. They foster the desire to get into print to the detriment of the sport. For example, if you cannot get up a climb then overcome this by using a piton for aid because you do not get your name into the magazines by failing. The other thing is that it takes me so much effort to write an article. I would rather it went into a journal, where it is kept historically, than a magazine which is thrown away! As for the money they offer, which is not much, I might just as well offer my articles to club journals. I am not interested in forwarding the interests of these magazines: any contribution I can give to climbing is free. The only proviso is that I direct where the article goes; it must not go to these periodicals.

D.G. I must disagree, for I feel that a good climbing magazine can fill a very useful purpose. Getting back to your climbing, do you consider that your hard routes of today compare with the climbs you were pioneering ten or fifteen years ago? Or do you feel that you reached your peak with climbs like *High Street* and *Astra*? Although your new routes now might be harder, is it just a fact that you have become more cunning?

A.A. Modern protection methods enable me still to climb at a high standard. If 1972 were 1955, I would have by now given up all thoughts of hard new routing. Dolphin thought he was at his peak at twenty-seven, and I agree with him. I do not think that a climber can climb past his youthful enthusiasm without good protection on routes. It is guts and stupidity which makes a climber lead hard bold routes, and you can only do that when you are under thirty. It's not a question of being married with a family; it is just that after that age you start slowing down mentally. Modern protection methods are like whisky: when you are going to try a hard move, you put a nut in. I would certainly not have been able to make the moves today which I did in 1955, regardless of how hard they are. Until your middle thirties your muscular ability is still good, but after that age, your peak performance begins to drop off, though your stamina might improve. Yet with the aid of the new protection devices you can still make hard moves, which can only mean in your earlier days you were climbing well below your top standard. The margins of safety then meant that one needed to rely on having good technique, and not to be bolstered by rope work and modern protection. My climbs of today are a lot easier to pioneer. Mentally, they only take me one tenth of the effort they once did. It has been years since I was frightened that I was going to be killed.

D.G. You have always been the absolute amateur, climbing mainly at weekends and during short summer holidays. Have you ever been envious of climbers like Bonington and Brown who have managed to spend so much of their time climbing? Do you think that professionalism with its inevitable train of commercialism will in the end be a very bad thing for the future of climbing?

A.A. I think professionalism is bad for climbing. Climbing is essentially a pastime and not a competitive activity, hence, the more that professionalism develops, the worse it is for our sport. Am I envious? If I had my time over again I would most certainly spend four years at a university, doing a subject that involves the minimum amount of work and a maximum of spare time. Expeditions: no, I am not interested in them. The effort involved seems to me to be so great I do not think I would enjoy it. The pinnacle of my desire would be a three-month holiday in the Alps.

D.G. Do you think that you will ever give up climbing?

A.A. I hope that I will always climb. I cannot say whether that will always be so. I will find it difficult to drop my standard, but I ought to be leaving a lot of easier routes to climb in the years to come. I think I will always climb. I hope to be like some of the old Fell and Rock club members, like the present president on his meet at sixty-five years of age. Borrowing a pair of rock boots to be taken up some Very Severes; that is how I hope I will be at sixty-five, borrowing somebody else's magic boots and being led up an Extreme climb.

D.G. Many thanks, Allan. I think we need to enlighten a new generation of climbers as to why *Ragman's Trumpet* was in your case so apposite, for your weekdays are spent working in the family business, as wool waste merchants (once a traditional activity in Bradford).

UPDATE: In later life, Allan, due to injury, turned away from climbing to sailing. His family opened an outdoor retail shop in Bradford, using his name as the identifier. Brian Evans was a founder, along with Walt Unsworth of Cicerone Press, which they sold on their retirement.

This interview first appeared in the 1973 *Leeds University Union Climbing Club Journal*; it was most recently published on *Footless Crow* in November 2020.

8

THE BARLEY BROTHERS

A family tree of any group of climbers, club or long-standing partnership will always have some surprising links, unknown to later generations.

Every two years around June my phone rings at home and a voice as near to cultured as we ever get from West Yorkshire, tainted by a slight Canadian accent, announces the arrival, keen to climb, of Dr Robin Barley. His brother Tony will be reactivated and dragged away from his high-powered business world, and for a few days the Barley brothers will be back in residence around their old haunts: Almscliff, Brimham, Caley, Kilnsey, Malham and, of course, Guisecliff. This last summer the act was repeated yet again and, watching them at Almscliff, with both still able to climb routes like *Wall of Horrors*, *Black Wall Eliminate* as well as boulder problems like *Crucifix Arête*, sets the memory processes to 'recall'. I suddenly realised that here were two of Britain's most accomplished climbers, each with an outstanding pioneering record, something I had not bothered to consider previously. Familiarity, I guess, is my reason for that, but such friendships are not to be downplayed: there is much to know and admire from the Barleys' story.

Robin and Tony, hailing from Nidderdale, are real Dales people. They started climbing, like so many of their generation, by fell walking in the Lake District: their parents owned an old caravan, parked under Bowfell's

Band, and there they spent many of their holidays. In 1960, when Robin was fifteen and Tony twelve years old, they started to climb in earnest on their own midden of Brimham Rocks. For a year they climbed solo, as they did not own a rope, but they still managed climbs up to and including Very Severe (not to be downplayed, shod in tennis shoes), using human pyramid techniques, both to get up routes and, if necessary, to effect self-rescues.

At this time, they were both at boarding school, Ashville College in Harrogate. During term time they only managed to climb on Sundays, at the only crag they could reach: Almscliff. They used to get out of church at 12.30, run to the crag (hiding their best Sunday suits in a forest on the way and collecting them on their return) and after climbing all afternoon race back in time for chapel at 5.30. This was illegal but it made Tony the best runner in the school by the time he was into his teens.

Eventually, Robin bought a 98cc James motorbike, which they kept at a friend's house and which Robin used to tow Tony to the local outcrops while he rode his push bike: even more illegal! They still had no rope, but after Robin had nose-dived off *Pothole Direct* at Almscliff in his new pumps, their father made them a 120-foot rope out of Italian hemp in the family spinning mill.

Using this secret weapon, they began to explore Guisecliff, which lies across the valley from their family home at Summerbridge. This huge and complex cliff (as outcrops go) is no place for those with weak stomachs: rotting sheep carcasses abound at its base, and it is the only gritstone crag in the country where machetes, mosquito nets and swamp fever are endemic. Guisecliff is jealously guarded by barbed wire, irate farmers (of which there are a lot in West Yorkshire) and dinosaurs.

The techniques that the Barleys developed there served them in good stead over the next two decades on crags as far apart as Africa and the Americas. They pioneered their first new routes at the outcrop in 1961 and have continued to explore and dig out rough diamonds ever since. That same year, 1961, they returned to holiday in the Lakes and found they could climb Very Severes without trouble on cliffs like Gimmer, but the exposure frightened them to begin with and took some time to get used to. They were still climbing on their hemp rope, but when it was not in use on the crags, it had to be stored away from human habitation, as it smelled strongly from its impregnation by Guisecliff crud.

Robin Barley (left) with the author. © Dennis Gray Collection

In 1962, they began to make a mark. Robin gained entrance to Manchester Medical School where he found himself in a hotbed of climbers and climbing activity, while at home Tony made the first free lead of *Comet Wall* at Guisecliff.

West Yorkshire is still parochial, but in that era it was positively a village as far as climbing was concerned. It was at the old Square and Compass pub (near Almscliff), in Tommy's cafe at Otley, and on the crags when climbers met and swapped stories that I began to hear about two young brothers who were burning up the area's hard routes, and that the elder, Robin, had pioneered a difficult new crack climb on an outcrop near Skipton called Raven's Peak. This we had to have a look at. Jeff Appleyard and I headed there at the first opportunity, despite it being a damp Saturday in November. It took our combined best efforts to crack the crack in question, and we were impressed. Shortly afterwards, I met Robin at Caley Crags on Otley Chevin, accompanied by a fellow Manchester student, Roger Mitchell. They had recently climbed *Vector* at Tremadog, which at that time had a high reputation for difficulty, with Roger shod only in plimsolls.

Unfortunately, shortly after this event, Roger suffered a horrific motorcycle accident which resulted in the amputation of an arm. He still climbs, cheerfully accepting his lot, but like so many others his was a climbing career of potential brilliance which through force of circumstance was never allowed to flourish.

At our first meeting, I was struck by Robin's gentleness. Dark, medium in height, good-looking and lithe, he seemed very self-assured, speaking quietly but knowledgeably, and though it was obvious that climbing meant an awful lot to him, medicine meant even more. Through Robin, I later met Tony, still a schoolboy, and so unlike his elder brother that it was hard to credit that they were from the same family. 'Powerful' is the best way to describe Tony: medium height, bespectacled, gingery, outspoken, but not brash. He was a keen sportsman – a runner, long-jumper and a rugby player.

In 1963, the brothers' climbing really began to flourish and they pioneered many new routes in West Yorkshire, the best being *Beatnik* at Brimham. Robin climbed this solo on the first ascent, having failed to top-rope it previously. Another outstanding lead by Robin at this time was the *North Wall Eliminate* at Guisecliff, a contender for anyone's list of the ten best routes on gritstone.

I climbed a lot with them during this period, in the Lake District and North Wales, making early repeats with Robin of routes like the *Cromlech Girdle, Deer Bield Buttress, Pellagra, Grasper* and others. One climb that stands out in my memory came on a damp day when Robin had set his ambitions on leading *Shrike* on Cloggy and was not to be denied, an impressive experience with the mists swirling and the rock greasy under hands and feet. But it was led without any fuss or shout, and with little in the way of protection other than spike runners. Although by this date we knew about nuts, they were thought by our own peers to be 'unsporting' and they did not gain universal acceptance until about 1966.

In June 1964, Robin and I paid two visits to Malham to investigate possible new routes. On the first occasion we climbed *Wombat*, and on the second *Macabre*. Both of these were among the hardest free routes of their period on limestone. At the crack on *Wombat* it was quite a task to place a chockstone big enough to jam in for protection, and on the final wall a heavy thunderstorm forced Robin to escape off right. I then climbed up the route on a tight rope in the rain, but later that afternoon Robin led *Wombat* after it had dried out and, seconding him, even in good conditions, it still felt like a difficult challenge.

Macabre was something else, for it was frighteningly loose and badly protected for both leader and second. The idea of attempting this line was Robin's. At the time I owned two hawser-laid ropes, one of 120 feet and the other of 150 feet of overweight nylon, the latter being an unusual length at that date. As Robin set forth, I assured him we were using the 150-foot rope. He climbed up the first wall, arranged some sketchy protection and then began some difficult moves, down-climbing, before embarking on a rising traverse leftwards. The rock was terribly loose, and at an overhang Robin placed a piton which, as the limestone crumbled around it, later popped out into my hand as I seconded the pitch. As Robin bridged across into a corner crack near the top of this first pitch, the pillar he was hanging from simply dropped out from between his arms. Somehow, he managed to stay in contact to reach a layback crack, but it was at this point we discovered the rope we were climbing on was my shorter, 120-foot version. My leader stayed cool, though, stuck as he was at the end of the rope, from which he untied and then retied back on to a lengthened strand which he had achieved by joining up all of his slings by knotting them together! Seconding the pitch, I was impressed with its seriousness: if Robin had fallen from any height, he would probably have been killed. If I had fallen on the first section, I too would have taken a ground fall. The second pitch was to be an anticlimax up a corner groove, composed of excellent, sound rock. *Macabre* is graded E3 now, twenty-two years after its first ascent, but that exposed beginning is protected by a ring peg on *Carnage* which did not exist at the time.

In 1964 I was away in the Himalaya from June, returning in January 1965. During that summer, Robin went out to the Alps with some of my friends from the Rock and Ice Club. They enjoyed a good season and managed several impressive ascents. Starting in the Dolomites, they moved on to the Piz Badile and finished in Chamonix, Robin's best effort being the north face of the Petit Dru.

On arriving home, Robin, inspired by our earlier successes at Malham, decided to start exploring Kilnsey Crag with a view to pioneering free climbs there. Accompanied by Tony, he set forth on the Central Wall, which had not been free climbed at that date. After totally committing himself, he managed the first forty feet without any protection to reach an old *in situ* piton but found he could not take his hands off to clip into it. He decided to grab hold of it. The offending piece of metal shot out and Robin hit the ground, fracturing both ankles, his lumbar spine and a wrist. Tony carried him down to the road, where they found that Robin couldn't drive their motorbike. Tony, being only sixteen, did not know how to! Their mother was summoned with a car and Robin spent the next few weeks in hospital, but as is the way with young people he soon recovered.

The brothers' most successful UK climbing year was perhaps 1965. Tony joined Robin at Manchester university. In the ranks of the mountaineering club were to be found many other luminaries of that period: Mike Yates, Geoff Cram, John Jones, Martin Boysen and several other outstanding climbers. Tony was by now one of the most forceful leaders ever to emerge from West Yorkshire, and when climbing with Robin they made up one of the five strongest teams in that era since Brown and Whillans, only equalled, perhaps, by Pete Crew and Baz Ingle.

They pioneered so many routes in the next two years that mere lists mean little. *Carnage* at Malham was a high point, climbed on a wet day with only two points of protection. *The Creation* at Guisecliff is a ferocious crack climb. At Kilnsey, *Trauma Traverse*, which although not a high-standard route was an important development because it was a free climb. I had ascended the first crack several years before but had finished in the gully.

For the next two years, until Tony's departure to work in South Africa, the brothers were active across the length and breadth of the UK, in the Peak, Wales, the Lakes and Scotland. Two of their outstanding climbs from this period were *Culloden* on Creag an Dubh-loch and *Rubberneck* at the Roaches, but it was in West Yorkshire they remained supreme. At Malham, they succeeded on routes like *Carnage Left-hand* and the *Blinds Finish* (climbed by mistake because Tony had forgotten the line he had followed on the first ascent), *Crossbones* and the *Right Wing Girdle*. At Gordale, they climbed *Yark* and *Yark Left-hand*, and at Kilnsey, *Warlord* and *Brainstorm*. On *Brainstorm*, Robin led the second pitch and appeared at its top above 'Fritz' Sumner who was nailing his way up *The Fly*. The latter nearly fell out of his etriers for to be free climbing at Kilnsey Crag in that era was unheard of. At Almscliff, Tony pioneered *Yellow Wall* and *Black Wall Eliminate*, and led the third ascent of the *Wall of Horrors*, where his only protection fell out as he moved up the crux flutings.

The summer of 1966 was a bad weather year in the Alps, so Robin and Tony fled to the Dolomites where they managed an almost-free ascent of the *Diedro Aste* on the Crozzon di Brenta. Back in Chamonix, still plagued by bad weather, on their way to climb the north face of the Chardonnet on the morning of his nineteenth birthday, Tony fell sixty feet down a crevasse. Robin managed to rescue him and they retreated to climb in Cornwall, but not before finishing the route.

In 1967, after graduating with a 2:2 in civil engineering, Tony went to work in Johannesburg and set about pioneering new routes in the Krantzberg and Magaliesberg mountains of the Transvaal. Climbing in Africa is always adventurous, particularly in dealing with the wildlife to be found on the cliffs there: vultures, monkeys and especially the baboons, snakes and bees; African bees are nothing like the tame specimens found in the UK and are lethal. In such remote areas drinking water can be a problem, while crossing rivers or swimming to cool down is dangerous because of such afflictions as bilharzia. Nor is there a vast number of climbers around, so one needs to be self-sufficient.

Tony revelled in such challenges, as did Robin, for in 1968 he finished medical school and joined his brother in South Africa. Over the next two years they pioneered fifty new routes, the hardest being *Armageddon* at Krantzberg, considered for over a decade the most difficult and serious climb in the Transvaal.

Robin was attracted to Cape Town, for it was there at Groote Schuur Hospital that the medical world was abuzz with the successful operation to perform the world's first human-to-human heart transplant. His move there led to major new routes on Table Mountain and he soon found that Cape Town is a rock climber's paradise. You ride to the top of Table Mountain on a cable car, then you walk down to the foot of your climbs where the rock is a sound, hard sandstone.

It was in South Africa that Robin and Tony pioneered their finest new route, *Apollo*, at Castle Rocks in the Hex River Mountains, probably the best hard rock route in the country. At 1,000 feet in length, it climbs through improbable overhangs on perfect rock. Tony also solved Table Mountain's 'last great problem' of that time, *Roulette*, the crux of which is an overhanging crack which leans out ten feet in twenty-five feet.

All of this successful activity was brought to an abrupt halt when Tony suffered a terrible accident on Mount Superior in the Hex River Mountains. Halfway up a 2,000-foot face, a ledge he was standing on suddenly collapsed and he fell about 200 feet, fracturing his skull badly and leaving him unconscious. Fortunately, his companion managed to lower him down the face, then with arriving help carry him to a nearby ridge where a helicopter evacuated him to Groote Schuur Hospital. This epic lasted for hours. It is a tribute to his physical strength that he survived the ordeal: once at the hospital, he clung desperately to life while the medical staff were still looking for heart donors. He pulled through, but only just – he was never such a bold or dynamic climber again.

By 1970, the brothers were back climbing in the UK. From there, they travelled to Norway, attracted by the Troll Wall, but the weather was foul. On a day when it actually did stop raining, they set off up the *Rimmon Route* at noon. By midnight they were above the Great Wall section, but it started raining again, which then turned to snow. They kept on climbing, because they had to. A desperate fight for life then ensued. They fought their way up the summit gullies, and by then, both were hypothermic through having to dodge avalanches, cascading water and rockfall. They topped out in a white-out and then had to walk back nearly all the way to Åndalsnes, for the road had been washed away. A twenty-four-hour round trip, but productive!

That winter, having married, Robin lived first in Sweden, then in Trondheim, Norway. In Sweden he developed along with local climbers the popular crags at Gothenburg, which are the Scandinavian equivalent of Tremadog and on which one of the test pieces is *Robin's Crack*, a fierce layback. At Helsingborg, he developed some impressive granite climbs akin to Cornwall. In Trondheim it was to be a heavy winter and the waterfalls there were all in good condition for ice climbing. Having brought Terror-dactyls from the UK, Robin started the winter climbing boom in that area. The locals of that period were not attempting such ascents until Robin's sojourn among them.

In 1972, Robin moved to Vancouver, where he lives to this day. He is a fellow of the Royal College of Anaesthetists and specialises in paediatrics. Living in Vancouver, it is possible to climb on Squamish Chief, which attains a height of over 2,000 feet and on which Robin has pioneered over sixty new routes, some of which rate among the highest quality routes on the cliff. Many required extensive gardening, and doubtless his apprentice-ship at Guisecliff stood him in good stead for these undertakings. In winter around Vancouver it is possible to ski, undertake long winter tours and at other seasons white-water kayak. Robin is more than just a dabbling participant in such activities.

Vancouver is a hub for travelling south into the USA, from where it is fairly easy to reach the climbing areas in California and Colorado.

In Yosemite in 1974, Robin, climbing with another close friend of mine, the late Bugs McKeith, who made such a mark on Calgary winter climbing, was below the pendulum on the *Salathé Wall* of El Capitan, leading into a difficult offwidth crack. Bugs had insisted that Robin lead this, as he was the man for such cracks.

'How on earth do you make that out?' enquired the doctor.

'Well, I was once at Almscliff with Dennis Gray, and you were there and so impressive soloing all those bloody horrible cracks!'

This puzzled Robin because he had never previously met the Scot, but then it dawned on him it was Tony who had been with us on that occasion, not him! This news rather shook old Bugs, for the only reason he had teamed up with Robin was because he thought that he would make short shrift of the desperate Yosemite cracks. In the end, Robin did keep up the family honour and led all the difficult crack pitches until the route was completed. He and Bugs became firm friends until the latter's untimely demise soloing in the Rockies.

Thanks to a year's sabbatical in 1978, Robin went to work in Africa once more, where he visited South Africa and Kenya, among other countries. Medicine fortunately knows no colour bars. While in South Africa he made a free lead of *Apollo* exactly ten years after the first ascent and pioneered some impressive new routes in the Cederberg.

Tony Barley has also kept active. In 1971, climbing with Ed Ward Drummond, he pioneered the *Moon* at Gogarth, and with Jerry Peel some difficult new outcrop problems. He is still to be found digging out new routes at Guisecliff in between the demands on his time posed by being a senior partner in a civil engineering firm. But he has also suffered some more of life's tribulations, including being struck by a virus which affected his central nervous system for quite some time. Once, while so debilitated, he came to visit me in my office at the BMC: it took him minutes to walk the last few yards from the car which had dropped him off. A year ago last Christmas he came and ran in our Boxing Day Chevin Chase race and finished last! But what an achievement, for the prognosis the year before had been that he might never be able to walk again. Fortunately, he did make a complete recovery and the following year he cruised round the course, despite the visible effects of too many business lunches.

It seems to me, writing about two close friends, that like so many other climbers they will always be looking for adventure and challenge in life.

Tony used to drive his car like a rally competitor and Robin is still into long ski traverses and kayak expeditions. They both became family men, each successful in their chosen professions. They have also both put something back into climbing, for Tony has been a long-serving member of the BMC technical committee, and Robin has held office in various climbing organisations, including being secretary of the Manchester university club when he was a member of that body.

The years go rolling by, and nostalgia may have tinted both the good and bad times with a rose-coloured hue. However, I do hope that for many years to come, every two years or so the phone will ring again at home, signalling the doctor's arrival from Canada and we can travel out together, to climb at Almscliff once more.

UPDATE: Tony Barley died on 17 August 2009, due to severe heart problems. He was however active almost until his demise, pioneering new bouldering areas above the Nidd Valley.

This article first appeared in *High* magazine in 1986.

9

WHISPER THE WIND:
JOHN SYRETT AND ROGER BAXTER-JONES

Whisper the wind around the rocky outcrop
Moving the long grass at the base of the Crag
Listen carefully to the noise it keeps making
Sighing and dying as it rises then falls

It tells of a warm day at the height of a summer
And the three young climbers who came here to play.
Their laughter remembered as I reach the rock face
Their faces I recall as I stand beneath the Green Crack.

These are the first two verses from a poem in my collection *From the Edge: Selected Poems* (Flux Gallery Press, 2012).* This poem was about a visit to Almscliff crag in the summer of 1969, with John Syrett and Roger Baxter-Jones. At the time, we were all studying at Leeds university, although, unlike the other two, I was a part-time student. Both of my companions subsequently made their mark on the history of British climbing, but both suffered tragic deaths. Verse three is intended to set the scene for how we felt and enjoyed our activities at that time:

---

* The collection was printed as a limited edition and it quickly sold out!

John Syrett at Earl Crag. © John Stainforth

But the wind is rising and I cannot now confirm
Just who led and who lay out bare back in the sun
We were happy then, for it seemed to be never ending
A life without strife with such good friends: it was fun!

Both John and Roger arrived at Leeds for the autumn term of 1968, John to read mineral sciences and Roger to study English. They were eighteen years old. They joined the university climbing club, which over the next few years was also to include other outstanding activists such as John Porter, Brian Hall, Alex MacIntyre, Bernard Newman, John Stainforth and a host of others.

John hailed from a village in Kent. When he arrived in Leeds, he was almost a novice rock climber but immediately settled to assiduous practice on the then famous university climbing wall. It seemed that any time you visited the facility, he would be there, and he quickly developed into one of its star performers. It is hard now to appreciate the standing of the Leeds wall in that era, with the massive developments that have subsequently taken place in such facilities, but it is fair to report that it was then the most important wall in the UK. Only fifteen feet high, it nevertheless boasted a hard landing, and some of the problems were very bold: not a few fractured limbs resulted from falls.

John's climbing style quickly developed as particularly adventurous: to watch him on his classic roof traverse at the top of the wall, laybacking on small undercuts with a fractured spine as a real possibility if he fell, showed real commitment. Nobody else in the early 1970s seemed keen to emulate the feat.

Thus, John was one of the first to realise what such wall training could achieve in developing rock climbing skills, and within a few months he was transferring these learned abilities on to the local gritstone outcrops. I first met him at the wall and in February 1969 arranged to climb with him at Ilkley. I had recently married. My wife and I were staying with my father in north Leeds while working to refurbish a weaver's cottage we had bought outside the city in Guiseley. Early on a Sunday morning, John arrived, having run five kilometres from his shared flat in Leeds 6. He was wearing flared jeans, desert boots and an open-neck white shirt, assiduously ironed and cleaned. In each hand he carried a PA rock boot, and that was all, despite it being an icy cold day with snow on the ground. My former wife Leni later remarked on John's startling good looks, being of average height, lithe, with sharply lit blue eyes, topped by a mass of thick, black curly hair. Pete Livesey noted his 'blue-eyed, god-like expression'. That first time climbing outside with John made me realise what a phenomenon he really was. Ilkley Moor is known for its biting cold, yet he spent most of the day soloing, wearing only his open-neck shirt and jeans while my wife and I cowered in our ancient Dormobile, sheltering from the elements and brewing up to combat the cold.

Over the next four years, John was to pioneer some of Yorkshire's finest routes. It was to be his golden period, with over forty new routes on grit-stone, such as *Joker's Wall* and the *Brutaliser* at Brimham, *Earl Buttress* at Earl Crag, *Propeller Wall* at Ilkley and some of Almscliff's outstanding test pieces: the *Big Greeny*, *Encore* and his eponymous *Roof* (still a 6b challenge), as well as one of the earliest repeats of the *Wall of Horrors*. Plus many more.

The companionship among climbers at Almscliff crag was palpable, their shared passion for the pursuit binding them together like a family forged by the rock. Each ascent, each moment spent on the rugged surfaces was imbued with a spirit of exploration and triumph over the elements. The evenings often ended with tales exchanged over pints at the local pub, laughter echoing through the smoky air as victories were recounted and challenges were dissected, creating an indelible bond among friends. It was a life rhythm marked by adrenaline-fuelled ascents and warm camaraderie, where the simplicity of the pursuit was its purity.

Most of John's new climbs reached the highest standard of the day, and although he tended to concentrate on the gritstone outcrops, his new climbs on limestone, such as *Midnight Cowboy* at Malham, were also challenging to the other activists of that period.

John graduated in the summer of 1972 and stayed on in Leeds: he seemed to be enamoured of the climbing, social and clubbing scene. I once saw him disco dancing at a climbing club dinner: he really was a mover! But disaster struck in late 1973, when at a drunken party he cut through the tendons on the fingers of one of his hands while opening a beer can. His climbing was never to be the same again, and though he continued to be active, he was to be limited by these injuries. He visited Yosemite in 1974 and spent the winter of that year in the Ben Nevis area, soloing classic routes on the mountain.

John remained in Leeds until 1978, but then moved to live in Newcastle where he embarked on a physiotherapy course. He continued to climb and pioneered an E4 5c on Northumberland sandstone, *Stella* at South Yardhope. Finishing his studies in Newcastle, he took up a position working on the North Sea oil rigs. A mutual friend, Mark Clark, who met him around this time, reported to me his worries about John's behaviour which he found to be concerning. John was erratic and drinking heavily: he was worrying about a fatal accident to one of his workmates, for which he seemed to believe he was somehow partly responsible, although an enquiry into the incident absolved him from any blame.

One weekend in June 1985, I was at Malham, and early on the Sunday morning a climber came running into the campsite to tell us there had been two accidents up on the Cove. Could we go and help? One of these was up on the Right Wing, so my companion and I headed up there to find a Scottish climber lying at the foot of *Wombat*. He had set off to solo this, but had fallen from low down. He was badly cut in the thigh, but with support he could stand. Between us, we helped him down the hillside and then to my car. As we moved away from the Cove, we met Pete Livesey who was heading up to help at the other accident. All he knew at that juncture was that someone had fallen from the top of the Central Wall of the Cove.

We drove the Scottish climber to hospital, where he needed several stitches to close up his injury. I then took him to where he could catch his transport back north. He assured me he would be OK doing this on his own.

After arriving home late that night, Pete Livesey phoned me with the terrible news that the body they had found at the foot of the Cove was John's. He had turned up at Pete's home in Malham the previous evening holding a bottle of whisky. They had drunk most of this while talking late into the night. John had then insisted on going off into the gloom to sleep at the top of the Cove. There is a large cave up there at its right side, and, on arriving, John was to find two other climbers in residence. He bedded down alongside them, but almost at first light he went outside, walked to the edge of the Cove and leapt off. Pete informed me that there was a note attached to his body: he had definitely intended to carry out this tragic action. He had taken the note to hand to John's relatives in confidence. Pete and I were good friends, and I agreed with him that this was for the best.

So ended the life of John Syrett in only his thirty-fifth year. A star that had burned so bright in his rock climbing career, but who set himself such high standards that when he could no longer meet these, his life moved on to what seemed to be an inevitable slow, sad demise. He remains, however, in my memory, forever young, and it is inspirational to recall the way he moved up a rock face.

The fourth verse of *Whisper the Wind* runs:

It is a long time though since we were here together
And alas it never can be again, for I am the only survivor.
The others were killed by their love of the mountains
Leaving me to grow old and trying to remember them.

Roger Baxter-Jones came from London. I first met him in late 1968 at Almscliff, where we ended by sharing a rope and climbing together. I was immediately taken by his extreme good humour and strong personality, which led to some of the other members of the university club to note that, 'It is all the way with RBJ.'

Roger Baxter-Jones in 1985. © Christine Baxter-Jones

Subsequently, I met him occasionally in the Pack Horse pub, the meeting place of the university climbers, but unlike John he was not a regular at the climbing wall, preferring to concentrate on spending time on a nearby dry ski slope, set up in an old chapel building on the edge of the campus: he eventually became a highly proficient off-piste skier. He was, however, a solid rock climber, but he would have been the first to admit that he could not emulate the outcrop feats of John Syrett, although they climbed several difficult climbs together such as the *Great Wall* on Clogwyn Du'r Arddu, with Roger in the lead, in 1970.

From his earliest climbing, however, Roger orientated himself to mountaineering. He had a powerful physique, was above medium height, but during his first Alpine season in the summer of 1969 he suffered a serious accident while climbing on the Piz Badile. This meant a long period of recovery and a drop-out from his studies at Leeds. On his return, he began to work in Centresport – one of the first climbing/skiing specialist retailers – and to teach dry-slope skiing, at which he had become highly competent.

Once fully recovered, he returned to alpinism, and from there on he accepted that this was where his all-round abilities were best employed. After summer successes, he began to also visit the Alps in winter. In summer 1972, he took part with me in hosting a BMC invitation visit to Snowdonia by a party of French climbers, which included such outstanding performers as Simone Badier, Patrick Cordier and Jean

Afanassieff. They made a big impression on Roger and were for him a boost to his growing sympathies for all things French.

He then studied at Sheffield and finally obtained his degree. A stand-out climb for him at the end of this period, in 1977, was the second ascent of the *Whymper Spur Direct* on the Grandes Jorasses with Nick Colton. And later still, the first winter ascent, solo, of the north face of the Aiguille des Grands Charmoz.

Over the next half decade, his life was dedicated to climbing in the Himalaya, commencing in 1978 with a bold alpine ascent of Jannu with Rab Carrington, Al Rouse and Brian Hall. In 1980, he attempted the south-east ridge of Makalu with Doug Scott and Georges Bettembourg. In 1982, he played a notable part in the successful ascent of a new route on Shisha Pangma, by its south-west face, with Doug Scott and Alex MacIntyre. In 1983, he summited Broad Peak with Jean Afanassieff, and he subsequently took part in two attempts to climb K2 in alpine style.

Back in Europe, he became more and more enamoured of the Mont Blanc range, in which region he became a leading exponent of first winter ascents, allied to his highly developed abilities in off-piste skiing. He also became a disciple of 'inner game' theory, a system of mind control developed by American Timothy Gallwey and adopted by some skiers as well as other sports enthusiasts.

Roger continued with his French odyssey, in language, tastes and attitudes. He became a Chamonix Guide, and in 1983 he married Christine Comte. He took French nationality while setting up the marital home with Christine in the Chamonix valley.

Old friendships remained, and that winter when my eldest son Stephen had an accident above Le Tour, Roger was the first to offer to help us. But following his dangerous calling, where he specialised in guiding experienced clients up major climbs, he was to die guiding the north face of the Triolet when a sérac broke away, obliterating all in its path, including Roger and his partner. The date was 8 July 1985, just one month after the death of John Syrett.

Trying to make sense of both John's and Roger's lives and deaths is difficult: they were outstanding personalities who eschewed conformity and followed their own paths. Few of us have the courage or ability to be so bold.

Here is the final verse of *Whisper the Wind*:

> *Whisper the wind around the outcrop*
> *Moving the long grass at the base of the Crag*
> *Listen carefully to the noise it keeps making*
> *Sighing and dying as it rises then falls.*

This article was first published on *Footless Crow* in March 2016.

PLACES

10

MOUNTAIN PAINTERS
AND SHAN SHUI

'The wise find pleasure in water; the virtuous find pleasure in hills.'

— KONG ZI (CONFUCIUS)

T he painting of mountains and/or climbing action is now an activity with a long history, but it is a difficult discipline to embrace in order to achieve a meaningful response for a studious beholder, and more so for the artist involved. In recent years there have been several such artists within the British climbing world, including John Redhead, Tim Pollard, Bill Peascod, Tom Price, Julian Cooper and Jim Curran, but they were, I believe, working within a subsection of landscape painting which has its historical origins in China, a form of art which has always encompassed a spiritual element, drawing on Daoism, but which only became explicit in the West with romanticism.

The earliest landscape paintings with no human figures depicted have their origins in frescoes in Minoan Greece, circa 1500 BCE, but by the tenth and eleventh centuries CE, during the Song dynasty in China, a form of painting with brush and ink – *shan shui* (mountain water) – had been perfected.

Mountains had long been considered sacred places in China; surprisingly, plains-dwelling literati painted vertiginous peaks, such as with Kuo

Hsi's *Clearing Autumn Skies over Mountains and Valleys.* These works included human figures set in the vastness of nature, with a Daoist emphasis on the insignificance of the human presence in a scene depicting mountains, waterfalls and rivers. These works – often in scroll form – do not try to represent an exact image of what the painter sees in nature, but rather what they thought about this. It is not important whether the painted colours or shapes look exactly like the real object, the intent is to capture on paper an awareness of inner reality and wholeness. *Shan shui* painters use the same materials and techniques as *shufa* (calligraphy); they are judged by the same criteria, including a philosophy which regards painting and *shufa* as a form of meditation, influenced by Chan (Zen) Buddhism.

During the Renaissance in Italy, the development of a thorough system of graphical perspective quickly became standard throughout Europe, and later in the United States, indeed eventually to an ever-wider geographic area. This allowed large and complex views to be painted, and these had a dramatic effect on the working of outdoor studies. Some of the most outstanding artists of the eighteenth and nineteenth centuries painted mountain scenes.

Crucial in this development was Caspar David Friedrich's *Wanderer above the Sea of Fog* (1818) which had a major influence on the Romantic movement, along with Thomas Gainsborough's *Mountain Landscape with Shepherd* (1783). Subsequently, in the United States during the nineteenth century, the White Mountain school arose. It later became the Hudson River school and included Albert Bierstadt, an outstanding painter of Rocky Mountain landscapes, and was associated with Thomas Hill, a recorder of views in Yosemite. By this time, mountain studies were appearing as far apart as Duncan Darroch in New Zealand (Mount Cook/Aoraki), Svetlana Kanyo in the Canadian Rockies, Sergio Lopez's paintings of Zion and the Sierras, and Ivan Aivazosky's of the Caucasus. Mountain paintings are such that they either complement one's taste and approval, or do not.

I have two favourite mountain painters, the English-born Edward Theodore Compton (1849–1921), and the Russian Nicholas Roerich (1874–1947). I was first intrigued by Compton's paintings when, along with Ian Howell, I was invited to give a talk in 1965 at the *Alpenvereinshaus* in Innsbruck about our 1964 attempt on Gauri Sankar. On the walls of some of the rooms were the most impressive mountain paintings I had then seen. I was even more intrigued by their provenance, and was informed they were the work of an English artist, E.T. Compton.

Compton, I later found out, had been born into a devout Quaker family in Stoke Newington in 1849, and exhibited from an early age an outstanding ability in drawing and sketching. His parents, recognising his unique talent, moved their family to Germany in order for him to study and develop his abilities, first in Darmstadt and then Munich. On a family holiday to the Bernese Oberland, he saw Alpine mountains for the first time and decided he would paint them. It was while living in Germany he began to climb: over the next five decades, he made over 300 ascents including twenty-seven firsts with some of the outstanding mountaineers of that era, such as Ludwig Purtscheller, Emil Zsigmondy and Karl Blodig. The latter was the first to ascend all the 4,000-metre peaks in the Alps. With Blodig, Compton made the first guideless climb, in 1905, of the Aiguille Blanche de Peuterey, and he also made first ascents of the Torre di Brenta and the south face of the Cima Brenta. In a German publication, *Berg*, he is described as physically strong and an excellent technical climber.

Compton became well known as an illustrator for the German and Austrian Alpine clubs and was the artist who provided the plates for two of the most iconic mountain books of that period, *Im Hochebirge* ('In the High Mountains') by Zsigmondy (1889), and *Der Alpinismus in Bildern* ('Mountaineering in Pictures') by Alfred Steinitzer (1913). In 1880, he was elected to the Royal Academy; he was also a member of the Alpine Club and the DAV (German/Austrian Alpine clubs). When he was seventy, he ascended the Grossglockner, but his climbing achievements pale when confronted by his canvases. His paintings of the Alps – he also visited North Africa, Scandinavia, the Andes and the UK, among others – including the Matterhorn, Mont Blanc and the Dolomites, are memorable, but his study of the north face of the Grandes Jorasses is peerless. This painting was exhibited in Chamonix last year, and all those many thousands who viewed this were impressed by its detail and accuracy, although Compton can still be regarded as an expressionist. He died in 1921; a hut in the Carinthian Alps bears his name, but his real memorial is his paintings. It has taken many years for his true technical and artistic ability to be recognised, but if you want to own one you now need deep pockets.

Nicholas Roerich, little known in Britain, is a man for whom the designation polymath is hardly adequate. There are two museums extant which illustrate his achievements as a painter, archaeologist, designer, writer, architect, philosopher, musician and spiritualist. There is one in New York and another in Moscow: both aim to illustrate the full range of Roerich's accomplishments, the most lauded of which are his paintings, particularly of Himalayan mountains and the peoples of those regions. The totality of his canvases spread among different collections around the world amounts to a staggering 7,000-plus paintings.

He was born in St Petersburg to a well-to-do notary public and studied law to please his father and art to please himself. He graduated from both university and the imperial art school with outstanding grades. An early interest in archaeology and history caused him to undertake a long journey through Russia, and from this, once a member of the artistic community in the Russia of that era, he developed a story, *The Rite of Spring*, with composer Igor Stravinsky. Serge Diaghilev had been a fellow law student with Roerich, and he invited him to design sets for the *Ballet Russes* which was to cause such a sensation in Paris before the First World War. Roerich's designs for Alexander Borodin's *Prince Igor* (1909) and *The Rite of Spring* (1913) cemented his reputation in that field.

During the Russian Revolution of 1917 – which he supported, along with Maxim Gorky – he was entrusted by the Soviets with the role of setting up an arts commission but, sickened by the killing and persecution which followed the revolution, Roerich migrated with his wife and two young boys first to Finland, then to England, having been invited by Thomas Beecham to design sets for him at Covent Garden. In England, he met H.G. Wells, George Bernard Shaw and Rabindranath Tagore, the Nobel-prize-winning Indian poet whose niece, the legendary Bollywood actress Devika Rani, married his youngest son, Svetoslav, in 1945.

During the first decade of the 1900s, largely influenced by his wife Helena, Roerich developed an interest in Eastern religions which would shape the rest of his life; the influence of Theosophy, Vedanta, Zen Buddhism and other mystical systems can be detected not only in his paintings but in the many stories and poems he wrote and illustrated. His wife was related to the composer Mussorgsky; another connection was with Rimsky-Korsakov. Because of these links, Roerich was invited to the

USA where he designed the sets for Rimsky-Korsakov's opera *The Snow Maiden*.

The couple settled in New York and founded an institute for the arts, an art school with an extensive and versatile curriculum, including architecture. Roerich's acclaimed publication on this subject, *Architectural Studies* (1904–1905), had become a standard text by that date. They also set up the Agni Yoga Society, while an exhibition of his paintings toured the country, and a book of his poetry, *Flame in Chalice* – translated by Mary Siegrist – was published at that time. The Roerichs stayed in the United States until 1923, but then travelled to Darjeeling, encouraged to move there to be near the Himalaya, which was where they felt their spiritual journey was leading them. One of Roerich's paintings of Kangchenjunga from this period has subsequently sold at auction for over £1 million. I have a framed print of one of these on my living room wall.

This interest in the Himalayan region led to the Roerichs setting forth with their son George, a brilliant linguist who was later to publish the first Tibetan/English/Russian dictionary, and six friends, to travel these regions for five years. They started in Sikkim, then moved on to the Punjab, Kashmir, Ladakh, the Karakoram mountains, Hotan, Kashgar, Ürümqi, Irtysh, the Altai mountains, the Oirat region of Mongolia, the central Gobi, Gansu, Tsaidam and finally Tibet. There, they received an icy reception, being stopped on the high Tibetan plateau, forced to live in tents in sub-zero conditions and to exist on subsistence rations for several months, during which time five members of their party died. Finally, in March 1928, they were allowed to leave Tibet, whence they retreated to India.

Returning first to Darjeeling, Roerich wrote several books about his experiences from this incredible journey, much of it on foot, two of which – *Altai-Himalaya* and *Shambhala* – were translated and then published in the USA. He had also painted many outstanding studies of the mountains he had viewed while traversing the Himalaya, including the Mustagh Tower.

In 1929, Roerich was nominated by the Sorbonne for the Nobel Peace Prize. His concern for peace resulted in his creation of the *Pax Cultura*, the 'Red Cross' of art and culture. His work for this cause resulted in the USA and the twenty other nations of the Pan-American Union signing the Roerich pact on 15 April 1935 at the White House with President Roosevelt. This pact was an early international instrument attempting to protect cultural property.

Pictures of Roerich at this time illustrate a tall, bearded, erect personality who might have emerged out of the pages of a Tolstoy novel. In 1935, on behalf of the US Department of Agriculture, accompanied by two of their scientists, H.G. MacMillan and James F. Stephens, Roerich led an expedition to Inner Mongolia and Manchuria. The expedition's purpose was to collect the seeds of plants which prevent the destruction of benign layers of soil.

During his journeying through the Himalaya, Roerich decided on the need for a Himalayan Institute, and, in January 1929, he and his family moved to the Kulu valley in Himachal Pradesh. On a site he had noted on his previous travels, and near the village of Naggar, he bought the Hall estate from the Raja of Mandi. His son, Svetoslav, who is now revered in India as one of its most famous artists and who studied painting with his father from a young age, declared, 'I have seen many countries, but I have not discovered a more beautiful place than the Kulu Valley.'

There, they set up the Himalayan Research Institute, 'Urusvati', a name which in Sanskrit means 'light of the morning star'. From this base, they set out on journeys into Lahaul, Spiti and Ladakh. At the institute, they studied local cultures, languages, the natural sciences and much more. Both Nicholas and Svetoslav painted local peoples and scenery, while his eldest son, George, a philologist who had studied at University College London, Harvard and the Sorbonne, and was fluent in Sanskrit, Pali, Hindi, Chinese and Tibetan, studied local dialects and languages.

The Roerichs continued their intense work in the Kulu valley until Nicholas died in 1947. While living at Naggar, Roerich was visited by both Nehru and Indira Gandhi; subsequently, Svetoslav painted their portraits which, along with that of a former president, Radhakrishnan, adorn the central Parliament Hall in Delhi.

Nicholas Roerich was a mystic, and an altruistic philosopher dedicated to the Himalaya and its peoples. He painted them as no one else has. He was a symbolist. Before his Indian sojourn, many of his paintings were of Slavic history and legend which some find 'disturbing'. H.P. Lovecraft, the cult horror story writer, referred several times to the 'strange and disturbing' paintings of Nicholas Roerich, especially in his Antarctic novel of 1936, *At the Mountains of Madness*. Nevertheless, one of these 'strange' paintings, the *Madonna Laboris*, sold for £7.9 million at Bonhams in 2013. So, to own one of these you would need even deeper pockets than if purchasing a Compton.

There have been so many books about the Roerichs that it is hard to understand why so few people have heard about them in the UK. A biography of Nicholas and Helena, *The Spiritual Journey of two Great Artists and Peacemakers* by Ruth A. Drayer, was published in 2014; while *Inspired by the Himalaya*, a photographic book by Ashok Dilwali inspired by the paintings of Nicholas, appeared the previous year. Several of Roerich's own books are still in a revised and recently published form. Even musical compositions such as the *Roerich Suite* by Juan Carlos Garcia are available to stream or download. Besides the two museums dedicated to his works in New York and Moscow, there are Roerich institutes in Mexico and Brazil.

It is obvious now that Roerich was ahead of his time: his spirituality, and his interest in Eastern religions and their philosophies perhaps anticipated the 'Beat' movement and its Zen Buddhist disciples of the 1960s.* Few have been able to bridge the gap in thought and interpretation as he did. He was also a ferocious worker: to carry on with all the creative activity he undertook, year in, year out, is truly impressive. Inevitably, within his huge oeuvre there are works which are substandard, especially within some of his writings, but at his best, he was an outstanding artist of the highest ability.

This article first appeared on *Footless Crow* in November 2016.

---

* Zen Buddhism is a fusion of Daoist and Buddhist beliefs. Daoism is the only religion to emerge from China, although Zen is a Chinese construct from the Tang dynasty (618–907). It is known as Chan in that country and Zen in Japan and the West.

11

FALAK SAR: THE ROAD TO HEAVEN

Falak Sar (5,918 metres). © Israr/Shutterstock

I n life sometimes, one comes to realise, years after what was a signal event, both how lucky and unaware you were that you were so close to the edge of an adventure that might have led to an early death. For me, this stuff of nightmares still surrounds a solo journey I made through Pakistan in the early 1990s. By then, I had visited the Himalaya several times, taking part in climbs and treks, and I felt confident that I could take off on my own to explore what was in climbing terms a relatively unpopular region. To do this, I decided to travel to Swat and explore the environs of its highest peak, Falak Sar (5,918 metres).

Before I explain what happened during this journey, some history and an explanation of Swat's place in Himalayan geography are needed. Swat lies west of the Indus valley and east of Chitral, and its mountains are an extension of the Hindu Kush. It is widely known as the Switzerland of Pakistan. Historically, it was a centre of Buddhism before the Muslim conquests, and in the Swat valley there are many reminders of this, including a large second-century Buddha figure, subsequently badly damaged by the Taliban. The eighth-century tantric master Padmasambhava, whose influence on the development of Tibetan Buddhism is central, was born in Swat. Known in Tibet as Guru Rinpoche, he was responsible for the first monastery to be built in the country, in the eighth century at Samye, and he founded one of the four major schools of Tibetan Buddhism, the Nyingmapa. Swat has also been visited by many other historical figures in its history, including, as early as 327 BCE, Alexander, and before him several Persian conquerors.

In terms of its modern story, the arrival of the fearsome Yusufzais, Pashtuns from Afghanistan who occupied Swat in 1515, is crucial. They challenged the British Raj forces on several occasions, including the Malakand uprising in 1897, an action made famous by Winston Churchill, then a second lieutenant in the cavalry, writing despatches about the campaign for the *Daily Telegraph*. Just like events that were to mirror these almost a hundred years later with the rise of the Taliban, the Pashtuns were driven in a religious fervour by a charismatic leader, Saidullah. However, during the Raj, Swat became a princely state ruled by a wali, and it remained so until 1969 when it was subsumed into Pakistan. The Queen and Prince Philip stayed with the wali at his white marble palace at Marghazar in 1961.

The Swat valley is wide and open at its southern end, but as you travel northwards it slowly climbs from 1,000 to 2,900 metres and narrows. The valley is approached from the south by the Malakand Pass and arriving at its base you realise why the 1897 campaign was so challenging and bloody. However, once into the valley it is a fertile, green sward to travel through, and in its lower reaches are apple and apricot orchards; it was once known as Udyāna, which translates as 'garden'.

A reason for my deciding to visit Swat arose from the pictures I had seen of its two highest mountains, Falak Sar and Mankial Sar (5,722 metres). They were depicted as impressive peaks, despite their modest heights in Himalayan terms. Falak Sar was first climbed by New Zealanders W.K.A. Berry and C.H. Tyndale-Biscoe in 1957, while R.L. Holdsworth and party ascended Mankial as early as 1940.

My journey to Swat began by catching a bus from Rawalpindi to Mingora. I spent a night there before travelling to Kalam, situated near the head of the valley. En route, I had been surprised to encounter men dressed in Greek-style clothing, some of whom had blue eyes and blond hair. Conjecture is that their antecedents arrived with Alexander, but once at Kalam I quickly realised I was in Pashtun country, dominated by the fearsome Yusufzai.

The Swat valley was as beautiful as I had expected, and in late summer its startling green hillsides and orchards were full of fruit. I stayed the night in Kalam in a cheap dosshouse, then set off laden by a heavy rucksack to climb the steep track that led towards the Ushu valley. As I ascended, Falak Sar came into view. I could see that its huge south face would be beyond me on my own, but I entertained a crazy notion of attempting the bounding south-west ridge. The south face route had been climbed in July 1990 by Hermann Warth and Sherpa Ang Choppal, overcoming twenty-five pitches of steep ice to reach the mountain's summit.

Ushu, situated on the Swat river, offered stunning views all around and appeared a restful place when I finally arrived there. However, I began to feel uneasy while moving around this village as its denizens did not appear to be too friendly. I could only surmise from their sullen looks that a lone climber was not only an unusual sight but also an unwelcome one. After a rest, I shouldered my pack once more and walked on. I spent the night higher up the valley near Matiltan, sleeping in a rough shelter and cooking on a wood fire from the plentiful supply left by its previous inhabitants. Early next morning, I was away swiftly to avoid the heat of the day, and for a few hours I made good progress. Coming from a recent climb in the Karakoram, I found no difficulty posed by the increasing altitude.

I was into rugged terrain by then, following an exposed rocky path along the steep sides of a gorge containing the Paloga river. As I balanced along, I looked ahead of me and noticed two tiny human figures, a long distance away but distinctly framed in the clear mountain air. At first,

I guessed they were shepherds, but the closer they descended towards me, the more uneasy I became. They were losing altitude at such a pace that I realised they could not be with any animals, and they must be chasing after something. Within a few moments, I realised that something was me. Panic set in. As they came closer, I saw they were both armed with Kalashnikovs, so even if I dropped my pack and tried to run off downhill I would not escape them. Though scared witless I decided to keep walking towards them while trying to remember some Pashto. When they did reach me, they were the two most frightening-looking characters I have ever met. Tall and bearded, they were dressed and looked like the mujahideen I had met on the Afghan border the year before, except they were more ragged, with rips in both their shalwar and kamiz.

'Salaam alaykum,' I greeted them as we met head on. Though surprised by my greeting, they did not give way, and I realised I was now their prisoner. 'Hello,' I gasped out in English while trying to smile at them, but the two did not seem appeased by this, and I froze with fear as one of these Pashtuns slung off his rifle, slipped its catch and pointed it at me. '*Ugud!*' I gasped out. 'I am going up into the mountains,' and pointed up to where I thought Falak Sar must be. '*Ugud!*' I repeated.

This brought the most unexpected response, for my two guards began to laugh loudly, then one of them cried out, '*Dodai!*'

I nodded my head, guessing they must think I was a hunter of some kind, but then I realised that this was what they were. They were not shepherds but had been out looking for game to shoot.

I began to laugh hysterically in relief at this, and my mood carried over to the Pashtuns who joined in with ringing shouts of mirth. The rifle that had been pointing at me was lowered and a hand was held out. I have never been so relieved to grasp a hand in my life. After sharing some naan bread, we parted in good spirits, they to continue their descent into the valley, I to continue climbing towards the base of Falak Sar. Some hours later, when I had reached high enough to see more clearly, I realised the approach to reach the peak's base and the face above were not challenges to attempt alone, at least not by me. Just before darkness I found shelter, below the snow level, and bivvied out on a long cold night.

I rose just before dawn to watch the sun rise on Falak Sar, revealing it to be a challenging mountain to climb from its southern aspect. It was an impressive sight, made all the more acute by being in such a remote place on my own. After cooking breakfast on a fire with some wood I had carried up from the valley, I repacked my rucksack and made ready to start back down the route to Ushu. I was worried what my reception might be on my return, for recent events had rather unnerved me. If I had known more about the forces that were then underway in the whole Swat valley and its future takeover by the Taliban, I might have been even more disturbed.

Descending to Ushu, I managed to cover in a day what had taken two on the way up, but apart from the two hunters I met no one else. With autumn now setting in, the mountains seemed deserted. Arriving in the valley, I was surprised to be met by a small group of local people, who on this occasion were friendly, unlike when I had previously stopped there. Partly by sign language, partly because he could speak a little Urdu and English, I realised that the *tehsildar* (headman) was inviting me to drink chai with him. Sitting in his hut, he laughed long and hard about his nephews having nearly shot me. They had fought in Afghanistan during the Soviet invasion, as had many Swat Pashtuns, and some of their relations had died in that conflict. They had thought me to be connected to one of the Soviet-supporting nations, and if I had not spoken to them in English they would have shot me. I realised how stupid I had been in not letting family and friends know about my plans to visit Swat. I could so easily have disappeared without trace, my body buried up in the mountains under a pile of rocks.

Subsequently, I realised that the Soviet–Afghan war had changed everything, not only in Afghanistan but in Pakistan's North-West Frontier Province. The involvement of the Americans and the Pakistan secret service in supporting and arming the mujahideen, as a part of the Cold War conflict, has led on, with the rise of Islamic fundamentalism and the Taliban, to an unstable situation that is still killing people in great numbers. It explains why in these areas so many of the denizens are armed: the year before my visit to Swat I was in Waziristan where every male seemed to be carrying an AK47.

In the 1990s, Swat began a nightmare descent into fundamentalism. A cleric, Sufi Muhammad, emerged and began to impose Sharia law on the peoples of the valley. By the 2000s, the Taliban had begun to take control. One of their targets was a ski development in the lower Swat valley at Malam Jabba, a joint project with Austria. The Taliban declared skiing as un-Islamic, and they decided to destroy this carefully constructed development. Thanks to the Pakistan army's move into Swat to deal with the Pakistani Taliban it re-opened in the winter of 2017.

There are approximately two million people living in the Swat valley, and in Mingora, its largest city, the Taliban committed their worst atrocities, with public hangings in its main square. It was in October 2012 that a young schoolgirl from Mingora, Malala, was shot in the head by Taliban gunmen for advocating girls' education. She was subsequently awarded a Nobel Peace Prize.

It's worth remembering that the Taliban was formed by Afghan Pashtuns who had studied in conservative Pakistan madrassas, like Mullah Omar and with the support of the Pakistani intelligence service ISI. Now, its former head in Swat is the leader of the Pakistan Taliban. The Pakistan army is still heavily involved here: over recent years the 'war in Swat' has been prosecuted with some success, but just like in Afghanistan, the Taliban are carrying out a further series of attacks on those people and organisations they decide are un-Islamic.

I believe as a climber that such events often seem unrelated to our mountain ambitions: we just wish to go about our activities peacefully, while respecting local peoples and their cultures appropriately, but the events on Nanga Parbat (8,125 metres) in June 2013 should make us aware that we are not now immune to events taking place outside our own bubble. The area around Nanga Parbat has always been politically complex. Because of the depth and scale of the four access valleys set around the peak, people living there were isolated from one another. They each speak a different language and seem distrustful of one another and outsiders.

This was brought into focus for me while leading a trip on the northern, Rakhiot side of the mountain, attempting to climb the Jalipur Peak (5,206 metres) on the eastern flank of this huge face. Retreating in bad weather, we crossed a pass by that name into the upper reaches of the Diamir to descend via the Patro valley, but were halted on the screes below the summit of the pass by gun-toting locals. They would not let us descend further unless we paid off our porters from Tato in the Rakhiot, employed them instead and paid a fee to camp in their valley. They were very aggressive, and it was obvious our Tato men were frightened by them. Fortunately, Hussein, our sirdar, could speak their language, Shina. In the end, we had no choice: the weather was awful and the idea of retreating back over the Jalipur pass was a no-no for our tired and dispirited trekkers. We did as they wished, paid off our Tato porters and then handed over a quantity of rupees in order to continue our descent.

Others can recount similar stories in the 1990s, including friends on the Rupal side of the mountain, but the events that occurred on the night of 22 June 2013 have no precedent in the history of Karakoram mountaineering. Fortunately, this happened in a period of good weather, and most of the parties attempting the Kinshofer route were above the base camp in the Diamir valley. Sixteen militants, dressed in the uniform of the Gilgit Scouts, guided there by a local, stormed the camp and proceeded to gather its eleven climbers and two base camp workers before them. They forced the climbers to hand over their valuables, money and mobile phones, which they proceeded to smash. They then made their prisoners kneel and began to shoot them one by one in the head. One extraordinarily brave Chinese climber, Zhang Jingchuan, broke free and ran into the night, followed by a hail of bullets, one of which grazed his skull with the effect that, as he ran, he was blinded by blood running into his eyes. Fortunately, below the camp, he dived into a ravine and escaped. Ten climbers from five different countries died that night, and one base camp worker. The second worker managed to convince the militants that he was a good Muslim and so they let him live.

The militants left early the next morning. The Chinese climber gingerly returned to the camp and his tent where he had hidden a mobile phone. He then climbed to camp 1 to alert climbers there as to what had happened. They managed to contact the Pakistani authorities, and shortly afterwards military helicopters arrived. Meanwhile, the climbers high on the Kinshofer route decided to descend, and eventually all assembled safely. Plans were made to walk out, but fears grew that the militants might still be in the area, and eventually everyone was airlifted to safety.

Obviously, such an event, which caused serious damage to the trekking and climbing industry in Pakistan, was truly significant and almost the next day questions were being asked in the country's legislature. An official enquiry was set up and a three-man team of an army colonel, a captain and a police officer were sent to the area, but they met a gruesome fate, gunned down by the Taliban in Chilas on the Karakoram Highway below Nanga Parbat. The climbers had erroneously claimed that they understood the attack was in retaliation for the killing of Osama bin Laden, but the Taliban claimed responsibility and said that it had been carried out because of a USA drone strike which had killed Wali-ur-Rehman, a local Taliban leader. Before the enquiry team were killed, they had managed to establish that the killers were local: ten from Diamir, three from Mansehra and three from Kohistan. Some of these were eventually tracked down and arrested under anti-terrorist legislation.

But questions remain. How could it be that the militants were dressed in Gilgit Scout uniforms? This irregular unit was originally formed by the British in the latter part of the nineteenth century, for the North-West Frontier Province was ever restive and Gilgit, the home of the Hunzas, who are Shia, were much favoured for this kind of soldiering. After Pakistan's independence, the Scouts were inducted into the country's army and eventually became designated the Gilgit Baltistan Scouts, with the task of keeping the peace in the whole of the province, which includes the Karakoram mountains. It seems to me that the attackers might really have been members of that outfit, for Kohistan is quite some way from the Chilas region, and how else would know each other? And what about the local guides who helped the attackers reach the base camp? Some reports advised there were two of them, others only one.

All indications were that in such climbing and trekking base towns and villages, like Hushe, Skardu, Gilgit and Askole, the locals were very critical of the Taliban action, for so many families had come to rely on trekking and climbing support as their source of income. It has helped to raise the standard of living and improved the infrastructure throughout the whole region. More recently, climbers and trekkers are returning, with security bolstered by a special mountain unit of the Gilgit Baltistan Scouts. For areas like the southern flanks of Nanga Parbat, they now accompany expeditions and remain in base camp.

For more than a century, climbers, explorers and trekkers have been enamoured of the Karakoram mountains. It is almost as if the natural forces have created a magical wonderland of peaks without parallel as challenges for climbers: K2, the Gasherbrums, the Trango Towers, the Mustagh Tower, the Latok peaks and so on. It is, I guess, certain that these challenges will continue to be met, but it is a good idea that such wider considerations as terrorism, its possibilities and actions be factored into future plans, for it is not going away from such regions any time soon. Clashes between Sunni and Shia, and attacks on Christians, are ongoing, and with the stand-off between India and Pakistan over Kashmir, which impinges on such areas as the southern part of the Karakoram range, I would suggest that all climbers and trekkers should keep a weather eye on these happenings before selecting an objective and a distant range to visit.

This article first appeared in the 2018 *Alpine Journal*.

12

IN THE LAND OF THE MORNING CALM

'Life is but a drop of water set in a boundless sea;
Go climb to the summits between heaven and earth.'

— YI-UN SANG

In 1984, I was invited by the Korean alpine club to run a course of instruction and explain to their leading mountaineers the training regimes then developing in modern rock climbing. This request was flattering to someone who was not even a Yorkshire first eleven – nor second for that matter – climber. But I was a member of the national coaches organisation in the UK and a board member of the association of British sports psychologists: I did know something about the subject, and so I accepted. Before I left the UK I tried to research 'climbing in South Korea' (there was no internet then), but I drew a blank, except for the fact that seventy per cent of the country was covered by mountains.

Arriving in Seoul, I was met at the airport by officials from the club and bundled into a taxi to the Bukhansan National Park, less than an hour from the centre of the city. There, at a road end, surrounded by Buddhist temples and steep hillsides, were granite faces and peaks. A forty-minute walk steeply uphill through the woods and I found myself arriving at a climbing hut, the base for the course, situated at the foot of a peak called Insubong, a 300-metre-high granite plug which could have been transported from Yosemite Valley.

The course ran for five days and thirty of the country's leading mountaineers attended. I use 'mountaineers' intentionally because at that date, with a few notable exceptions, that was where the Korean focus had been: many of the attendees had climbed in the Himalaya. So modern rock techniques, particularly in the protection of climbs, bouldering and specific fitness training were hardly on their horizons. Over the days of the course this is what I concentrated on, backed up by lectures in the hut in the evenings.

The Koreans' enthusiasm knew no bounds: we climbed routes on Insubong and bouldered on the superb blocks around the hut for many hours each day. I wish, however, to concentrate on the events which happened after the course was completed, and after I had attended as a representative of the BMC, the general assembly of the UIAA, held that year in Seoul.

The Chouinard route on Insubong. © Dennis Gray Collection

Shortly before the end of my stay, there appeared at the hotel where I was staying a motley group of Korean climbers I had not met before. It transpired they were the members of the Ahgoo Club. This translates as the 'Rock and Ice Club'. And as a member of that group in the UK, they immediately struck a rapport with me. They had come to invite me to go climbing with them. I accepted, despite some of the members of my course advising me against doing just that, the reason being, as I guessed later, that they were totally unconnected with the climbing establishment.

The Ahgoo arrived the next morning at the swanky Sheraton Hotel in a battered old minibus, and as I climbed aboard I regretted my temerity of the night before, for I had not been to bed and my head was throbbing like a beehive. The Koreans are known as the Irish of the East: they had certainly lived up to that sobriquet at a farewell banquet and subsequent carousing held the night before in downtown Seoul. The members of the Ahgoo Club made their living in the family co-operative producing outdoor equipment. Mums, wives, girlfriends all worked at sewing machines in the front room making rucksacks, clothes and sleeping bags, while the men hammered and filed away at the rear of the house manufacturing climbing hardware. In the communal Ahgoo van I was introduced to the members: everybody was called Mr Lee, except for Mr Wook, who had the best climbing record in the country. He was dark, in his late twenties and a bit portly, bigger physically than the rest, with shoulders and arms like a weightlifter. He had been to the Alps, once, and had climbed the Walker Spur of the Grandes Jorasses, the north face of the Eiger and the north face of the Matterhorn, the only three routes he had a description of in Hangul, the Korean written language. He had led a new route on the Ogre in the Karakoram, and he had visited the USA and led some of the hardest free climbs of that era on sight, some of them 5.12c, thereby impressing the Americans. And he had an extraordinary training routine, drinking several bottles of the local liquor a day.

We arrived at their 'factory', their home, and I was impressed by the industry that was going on there. Everyone was hard at work making equipment, but they stopped labouring at their tasks while they showed me a video of their Ogre climb. They had been to the mountain twice in successive years, 1982 and 1983, and on the first occasion they had been beaten back by bad weather and a serious accident, when one of their party had been swept away by an avalanche. The youngest member of the party, Mr Lee, who was the only one who could speak any English, explained, almost in tears, how this had happened, and how he and Mr Wook had dug his elder brother out as quickly as they could only to realise it was too late. I realised while watching the video that their leader must be something really special, for Mr Wook had led some of the hardest rock and ice pitches then climbed in the Himalaya.

After the video was finished and having said goodbye to all the family members, we headed for Dobongsan, a mountain to the north-east of Seoul. The area was similar to Insubong, but it was nothing like as popular, either with tourists or climbers. It was Mr Wook's favourite mountain, and on the face of Seoninbong he had pioneered the hardest pitch in South Korea, which he offered to climb with me. We climbed some boulder problems on the way up to the face, and it was immediately obvious that Mr Wook was a stronger climber than anyone who had been on my course. We then climbed a single-pitch route on a small crag below the mountain, to clarify our rope work and calls before venturing on to the bigger face above. It is hard to climb with someone who you have never met before and with whom you have not one word of common language.

The young Mr Lee was rushing about at full speed, up to the top of the crag and then back down again, while I explained 'slack', 'tight' and, if necessary, 'pull!' The rest of the Ahgoo were enjoying this and laughing out loud, while I struggled up the short but difficult climb, which I later discovered only Mr Wook had ever managed to lead.

The ascent of Seoninbong was tremendous: Mr Wook's hard pitch proved to be a direct finish to a classic, 300-metre 5.9/5.10 climb. An easy first pitch was followed by a superb undercut flake-crack, trending rightwards across the face, which my companion led with a minimum of protection. On his feet he wore a pair of home-made rock boots with sticky soles which he himself had developed. He protected the climb as he ascended by placing the odd camming device which he had also made himself in the cooperative. The next pitch was the hardest on the original route, and after leading a thin traverse I swung into a wild offwidth and nearly fell out of it. I had little in the way of protection and, as I climbed higher, I realised Mr Wook was shouting to me to turn around and face the other way. I caught a glimpse of him jumping up and down and gesticulating in a turning motion. This was not going to be easy, but facing left there was nothing to help me exit out of the top of the crack. My right arm was locked across the crack, and my right leg sunk deep inside. I was tiring fast and becoming desperate. I shouted to Mr Wook, 'Watch me!', but he just kept waving his arms wildly in the air. I held my breath and just as I was about to part company with the rock face, I did a swift about-turn, whipping my left arm, left side and left leg into the crack just as I began to slide out. 'Bloody hell!' I shouted to the uncomprehending Mr Wook. 'It's easy this way!' There were big holds on the right-hand side of the fissure.

After that excitement the climbing was straightforward until we arrived at Mr Wook's direct finish. I was impressed: a thin finger crack split the wall and disappeared from view about twenty metres above my head. I quickly made it plain to Mr Wook that I did not wish to try to lead it. He seemed unconvinced, but once I had tied myself down to about three belays he got the message and started out to lead it. 'Dramatic' is perhaps the best way to describe his ascent, as he made progress by finger and toe jams, in some places hanging clear on his jammed fingers alone. Once again, his home-made cams did good service in protecting this climb, and in following I had to admit I could not have led the pitch, which was 6a/6b climbing through-out, and probably a standard harder than any other then extant in the country.

We descended the face by a succession of abseils, and once back at the base of our climb I was surprised when Mr Wook pulled a bottle of liquor out of his rucksack. He offered me a slurp, but when I declined this offer he seemed genuinely surprised. He shook his head and proceeded to drain a large part of the bottle as if he was drinking water. Such a training diet would kill most other climbers.

I kept in touch with some of the Korean climbers after this visit, and a party came to the UK in 1988. But Mr Wook unfortunately was not with them or any of the Ahgoo. I returned to the country in 1992 and climbed again in the Bukhansan National Park, and at Masan and Pusan, and finally in the Seoraksan National Park in the north-east of the country, an impres-sive range of granite peaks and walls with great climbing objectives in summer and winter. Korean winters are really cold.

The climbing scene had changed massively in the eight years between my visits. There were climbing walls in all the main cities, and standards had risen dramatically. The number of climbers had more than doubled and the Korean Alpine Federation, similar to the BMC, claimed a membership of over a million activists. I never managed to contact the Ahgoo climbers again, for being outside the mainstream, nobody seemed to know much about them or their achievements.

This article first appeared in *Climb* in 2012.

13

BELGIUM: A COCKPIT IN THE DEVELOPMENT OF MODERN ROCK CLIMBING

B elgium – land of beer, chocolates and waffles ... and rock climbing? If you were asked which country had played the most part in the development of modern rock climbing, perhaps you would settle on the USA, France or even Spain. It is, however, unlikely that you would suggest Belgium. But, if uninitiated, history might surprise you if you did.

We used to drive through the country to reach the German motorway system and on to the Eastern Alps and the Dolomites, but on the way home in 1965, Margery Ann Thompson and I stopped off to climb in the Ardennes, at Freyr. This is the largest of the limestone cliffs in the range, seventy metres high, and now a site that boasts over 700 routes at all grades. We had a memorable time, climbing and socialising on that first visit, camping with dozens of enthusiasts from Holland and Belgium on the Club Alpin Belge site at the edge of the outcrop.

We made friends with Marcel Gailley, who hosted a bar and hotel in the nearby village of Falmignoul. At the time, Marcel's was a place where climbers would congregate in the evening. One of the topics I overheard there was about a recent visit by the famous French guide Lionel Terray, who was guiding a client at Freyr. Challenged for his opinion about the Maestri claim to have made the first ascent of Cerro Torre, all he would observe was, 'If Egger and Maestri had made this unbelievable first ascent, it was the greatest feat in the history of mountaineering!' This comment, often repeated, has real standing, because Terray had made the first ascent of Fitz Roy and was one of the few mountaineers who at that time had climbed in Patagonia, in the same range as Cerro Torre. Unfortunately, Terray died climbing in the Vercors a few months later.

After that first visit, I was keen to return to the Ardennes, and in 1968 the chance came to visit a place written large in the history of the area, Marche-les-Dames, when Dave Musgrove and I were invited to attend an international meet held at these rocks. Climbers from many countries took part. The usual adventures and alarms happened at this gathering: litres of Stella Artois were drunk in the evenings, and a big fall was taken by one of the participants from Holland who was immediately referred to as the 'Flying Dutchman'. Dave was caught on the lead by a sudden downpour on a route called *Les Cinq Ânes* and was saved by a MOAC slotted in a crack above him. We were subsequently invited to a vodka party organised by the Poles and Czechs.

But why is Marche-les-Dames so well known in Belgium? It is the training centre for Belgian commandos, and if it was not for another historic event, that would probably be reason enough. But what happened there in February 1934 stands out. The Belgian king, Albert I, a keen climber with a record of ascents in the Alps and the Ardennes, was killed while solo climbing on a pinnacle, the Roche du Vieux Bon Dieu ('Good old god'), a part of the Marche-les-Dames outcrop. The king was fifty-eight and an experienced climber, and the whole event led to conspiracy theorists having a field day. His valet was waiting in his car and eventually managed to gather together a search party from the local villagers. After many hours of searching on a dark night, they found the body in the valley below the pinnacle. It is thought that, nearing the summit of the pinnacle, the king pulled up on a hold which fractured, and he tumbled first on to a ledge below him, but slid off this, falling another twenty metres. A surprising feature of this accident was that the king had tied a rope around himself.

What gave the conspiracy theorists such a platform was the prestige the king had won for himself during the First World War. Although he was a cousin of the kaiser, he had refused to allow the Germans free passage through his country to attack northern France. He had remained active throughout the conflict and was known to his fellow Belgians as the Knight King. One can find on the internet many wild theories as to what really happened to Albert I. One was that he was murdered elsewhere, and his body secretly dumped at Marche-les-Dames. One of the wildest is that the Nazis had him killed because he had not sided with Germany in the war. Another of these theories runs to many pages. But, in 2016, at the University of Leuven, some bloody leaves that had been gathered by villagers at the scene of the accident and kept safe for all these years were analysed and the DNA compared to two distant male and female descendants. The blood on the leaves was shown to be that of the king. There is a very fitting memorial at the outcrop to Albert I, in the form of a large arboreal letter A and a plaque noting this accident.

Leopold III succeeded his father as king. He was also a climber and active in the Ardennes and the Dolomites. I have made an ascent of one of his major climbs, the Campanile di Brabante on the Civetta. He made this difficult first ascent in 1933 with Domenico Rudatis and Attilio Tissi, two legends of Dolomite pioneering. Leopold was ahead of his time, for he had the world's first artificial climbing wall built on the royal estate at Stuyvenberg in 1937. Designed by the well-known Bavarian climber Hans Steger, who spent six months living in Brussels superintending the construction of this facility, the wall is still there and pictures of it can be found on the internet. Compared to the earliest walls in the UK, it is far more like a natural outcrop, with challenging cracks, a wide chimney and steep walls obviously climbed by using small in-cut holds.

Unfortunately, the Second World War intervened but, unlike his father, Leopold allowed the Nazis to blitzkrieg his country, occupying and moving south into northern France, his reasoning being that the Germans had such a superiority in arms that it was pointless to resist. His government fled to France and he was imprisoned by the Germans, during which time his conduct did not endear him to some of his fellow Belgians. Following a ten-year imprisonment and exile, he returned to Belgium in 1950 and abdicated the throne the following year.

With my wife to be, Leni, we visited Marcel's at Christmas 1968. It was bitterly cold, but, with Jean, Gailley's son, I made a climb on l'Al Lègne, the highest of the buttresses at Freyr. Jean and his friend Paul visited us in 1970 when we were the wardens of Brantwood, near Coniston in the Lake District. They did some climbing on Dow Crag, making first Belgian ascents, and joined in with our 'big swim' across Coniston Water which we used to undertake at the end of a course.

In November 1969, I was invited by the Club Alpin Belge to undertake a lecture tour, starting in Brussels, then including Liège and talks at venues near Namur and Antwerp. I was impressed by the numbers attending, particularly in the two big cities.

In Brussels, I stayed at the apartment of Dolomite climbing legend Claude Barbier. Relatively unknown in his own country, in north Italy he was *Il divino Claudio*. I had first met him in 1959 at the Tre Cime di Lavaredo. Even by that time he was a well-known figure, having made the first solo of the north face of the Cima Ovest. In 1961, he climbed solo and in a single day the five north faces of that range, comprising 2,000 metres of ascent. Over the following seasons he made over 160 solo climbs, and 600 ascents overall. Many of these were the best-known climbs on the Civetta, Marmolada and the Brenta. He had also made several first ascents climbing with such partners as Reinhold Messner, and made the second ascent of the *Philipp–Flamm* on the Civetta, then regarded as the hardest free climb on the mountain. He had climbed the *Bonatti Pillar*, soloed the north-east face of the Piz Badile and, the year I stayed with him, the Walker Spur of the Grandes Jorasses, on which, with his partner, he had survived a storm and several forced bivouacs. He openly confessed that he did not enjoy such climbing. He favoured Dolomite climbing, and he spent every summer there.

I guess we would say he was from an upper middle-class background, and although at times money was a real consideration for him, he relied on his parents to fund his climbing, since he was not sponsored in any way. In winter, he climbed in Belgium, and over the two days I was with him, we climbed at Dave and Freyr. I found him a challenging person to be with, for he did not seem to relax, and his approach was more serious than other outstanding climbers of my experience. He was slightly above medium height, dark-haired and thickset physically, but he moved quickly and with power once on the rock face. I was impressed by his command of languages, for he was fluent in French, Dutch, English and German.

Although he had dropped out of university to climb, he was a real bibliophile, and his love, besides his climbing, was books: he had a very impressive library. He also was a fan of what we call modern rock – Pink Floyd, the Rolling Stones and, most of all, Johnny Hallyday. He was keen to talk with me about the Alpine Climbing Group since I had been its secretary, and he was one of only two persons ever to become an honorary member. He wished to form a Belgian alpinists' group, similar to the French Groupe de Haute Montagne of which he was also a member.

One piece of advice that Claude offered me was to watch out for the Flemish climbers. They were too liberal about beer drinking, although the people who looked after me in Antwerp had similar observations to make about the Walloons! From these remarks I learned something of the competition that exists between these two groups.

Claude had started to cut down the aid on some of the classic climbs at Dave, Freyr and other cliffs; he started painting pitons yellow since he felt they should not be used on ascents. This was seen by some of the other Belgian climbers as a controversial act, even arrogant. In May 1977, at the BMC, I was to learn via a phone call from Belgium of Claude's death in a climbing accident. Hanging on a caving ladder, he had been gardening, cleaning and preparing a new route on a cliff called Yvoir, near Namur. As it was midweek, no other climbers were around, but when he failed to meet his friend Anna Lauwaert she visited the outcrop and found him at its base, wrapped up in the ladder, having fallen forty metres. He had been killed outright. Immediately, the conspiracists began to theorise, even suggesting there had been foul play. There were obviously plenty of good belays at the top of this cliff: a tree, a metal fence and roots, but the two karabiners on the head of the ladder remained closed. One of the new routes Claude had pioneered in the Dolomites was named *La via del drago* ('The way of the dragon'), which became the title of the biography Anna Lauwaert eventually wrote about his life and climbs.

In the 1970s, I continued to visit the Ardennes, and one occasion was the nearest I came to a serious accident. Some of the routes on Freyr are approached by abseil, and my companion had set up one of these. I started out to lower myself over the edge but the next moment the rope was pulling free and I began to fall. Luckily, this was at the head of a groove in which there were some good handholds, and as I began to fall I grabbed hold of these and somehow stopped myself. 'How the hell did that happen?' It transpired that in setting up the abseil, through two *in situ* pitons, my companion had slotted the rope through the same loop of a short tape sling he had threaded into them. As soon as I loaded this, it pulled: a close call for me and sincere apologies from my companion.

From these visits it was obvious that climbing was becoming ever more popular in the country, but few outside Belgium would have expected that a development there would change how rock climbing would develop around the world, including in the UK. *Terres Neuves* ('New Lands') opened in Brussels in 1987; it was the first modern climbing centre in the world. In a large warehouse-type building, plywood was used to build walls on which were attached plastic holds in different colours: red, blue, yellow, white and so on. It was of course possible for routes to be set at different grades. This was immediately successful, and within months centres began to open in several other urban sites in Belgium.

In 1989, Jerry Moffatt, along with British climbing wall aficionado Graham Desroy, visited an old friend in Belgium, Arnoud T'Kint, who was working at one of these centres. Jerry was impressed by this and made a lot of videos of the action. On returning to the UK, he showed these to Paul Reeve and to Mark Vallance, the head of Wild Country, who both agreed to join him and to work towards opening such a wall in this country. In 1991, the Foundry opened in Sheffield, the first modern climbing centre in the UK. It has now led to many hundreds of such walls across the country. Some are for bouldering only, others are both lead and bouldering, but as they have developed they have become more and more sophisticated. This in turn has led to new careers in wall design and construction, route setting, wall administration, instructing, retailing at the walls, health and safety, and competition management. A whole new industry has developed, providing many work opportunities. An entirely different world from the natural environment in which the sport of rock climbing originally developed, but many of those involved in the wall developments have that kind of background.

Climbing is still a risky activity, less so at centres, and no one can tell exactly where this will lead next, especially as this style of climbing is now a recognised Olympic discipline. Many of those starting out on walls still wish to experience climbing outdoors; that is, I hope, in their best interests. But I think what I have written above makes the case for the importance of developments that took place in Belgium. It remains the only country in the world where its king has died while climbing!

This article appeared first in the 2023 *Scottish Mountaineering Club Journal*.

OPINIONS

14

TRESPASS

'Freedom is not a battle you fight for only once and win.
It goes on forever ... forever!'

— BENNY ROTHMAN,
LEADER OF THE 1932 KINDER MASS TRESPASS

Without access, climbing and hillwalking cannot take place. The access we enjoy today was hard fought for in a campaign that lasted over 150 years. Much has been written and discussed about the 1932 Kinder Scout trespass, and one of my valued possessions, presented to me by Benny Rothman, is a copy of its leader's view of the event published in an expanded A4 paperback format in 1982. I became friends with its author in the 1980s: he had become energised in that decade to campaign for continued access to water authority land after the privatisation of those bodies.

Benny was by that date a genial and persuasive character, barely five feet tall, a pocket Hercules, but one can imagine that in 1932 he was a fire-brand. An investigation into the social conditions then obtaining among the working class would make anyone understand why. There was mass unemployment, while such work as there was often smacked of exploitation and degradation; the living conditions were mostly set within poor housing and poverty.

So much of the British story is one of immigration, and Benny Rothman's was a part of that, for his parents were from Romania. Hundreds of Jews left the country around the turn of the nineteenth century, and Manchester is where his father Isaac fetched up, becoming a market trader running hardware stalls at Glossop and Shaw markets but residing in the then predominantly Jewish district of Cheetham Hill. A high-grade student, Benny won a scholarship to Manchester Central High School, but tragedy struck when his father died suddenly, forcing him to leave at fourteen to earn a living to help support his bereaved family.

Benny found work as an apprentice in the motor trade at a garage in Deansgate. One of his older workmates, a Scot, Bill Donne, invited him to attend the Sunday economics debates in the Clarion Cafe in Market Street. The Clarion movement originated in Manchester in 1891, fired up by a radical newspaper; it led to the formation of cycling clubs, rambling groups, choirs, handicraft groups and so on. It had more to do with the trespass movement to win access to, 'mountain, moor, heath, down and common land' than has so far been recorded, for a trespass in 1927 which was held in Derbyshire's Winnats Pass was organised by the Sheffield branch of the Clarion Ramblers. Benny, while an apprentice, studied at evening classes in the Manchester YMCA, but by 1927 he had joined the Young Communist League where a part of their activities was camping and rambling. Then sixteen years old, he built his own bike from spares and cycled to North Wales to climb Snowdon. From then on, he was a keen outdoorsman, eventually to become a leader-organiser for the British Workers' Sports Federation (BWSF).

The BWSF was set up by the National Clarion Cycling Club in 1923, and originally it was closely aligned with Labour, but over the following years it became disenchanted with the slow progress in improvement to access, and so by 1928 it had become a wing of the Communist Party of Great Britain. The Access to Mountains Bills had perennially failed, in 1884, in 1908 and in 1926, defeated by the landowning lobby, so one can understand the frustration this must have engendered among the rambling and climbing fraternity.

Labour then set up a competing organisation, since many in the access movement retained their links with the party. The Manchester Ramblers'

Federation, made up of over a hundred affiliates, refused to support a Kinder trespass, for it was to be held under the auspices of the BWSF, made up of a much younger membership who were less experienced in dealing with the authorities. To be fair to those who opposed the ramblers and climbers, in 1929, Prime Minister Ramsay MacDonald had set up a national parks committee, and the resulting Addison report in 1931 had recommended setting up a national parks authority to select the most appropriate areas to be so designated. The 'northern moors', however, were to be strictly preserved for grouse shooting. The worry of the older established outdoor organisations about a Kinder trespass was that it would set public opinion against open access to the countryside and the formation of national parks. But the depression and a change of government meant in any case that such initiatives were put on hold.

So how did the idea of a Kinder trespass germinate? At Easter 1932, the BWSF organised a camp at Rowarth, and from there a party set out to tramp over Bleaklow. They were to be met near Yellowslacks by a party of aggressive gamekeepers who turned the group around to return whence they had started their climb. This rankled, and the participants in the Bleaklow event realised that if there had been many more in their party, they could by sheer weight of numbers have overcome the keepers' demands.

Kinder Scout was selected by the members of the BWSF for a trespass because of its history and standing. It was the most extensively forbidden of the Peak District mountains, a part of the Enclosures Acts from the eighteenth and nineteenth centuries which had parcelled out public lands to private landowners, and it had become one of the most exclusive landscapes in Britain, preserved mainly for grouse shooting.

The would-be trespassers then began to publicise their event, particularly in the Manchester newspapers, in the *Daily Worker* and in the cafes and pubs around Hayfield. This was mostly the work of Benny and a seventeen-year-old from Salford named Jimmie Miller, who later morphed into the legendary songwriter Ewan MacColl.

Sunday 24 April 1932 dawned clear and bright, and by midday Hayfield was abuzz with ramblers, hundreds of whom had turned up to take part in this act of defiance, the Kinder Mass Trespass. As they were being contained by a heavy police presence and to get things moving, after a quick meeting of the BWSF personnel present, word went round to start moving. Out from Hayfield, first on to the narrow Kinder Road leading via White Brow and Nab Brow, passing by the Kinder reservoir into William Clough and eventually on to the plateau: but on the Kinder Road was a convenient abandoned quarry and the march was halted there. Although originally it had been planned for someone else from the BWSF to address the crowd of trespassers that had swelled to more than 400 participants, the person to do this had put in a no-show, and so Benny, a twenty-year-old, was called on to speak to this audience. Standing on a natural rock platform set out from the quarry sidings, he began his address with a plea for a peaceful demonstration, then went on to outline the history of the access movement as he then understood it. Finally, a system of whistled signals was agreed, and Benny's close friend, Wolfie Winnick, led the marchers off again.

I write that there were about 400 trespassers, but that was only the number scrambling up William Clough. Once on the plateau they met other groups, mainly from Sheffield, who had ascended from Edale. Before this happened, as the mass of ramblers turned right, they spread out widely in William Clough before gaining the Kinder plateau. There, they met a line of about thirty gamekeepers armed with sticks.

Though the majority of ascending bodies moved on and gained their objective, a small group did have a physical confrontation with some of the keepers. One who lashed out with his stick picked the wrong guy, a well-known amateur boxer who gave him a thump on the chin to make him think again, while a temporary keeper, Edward Beever, who had been threatening, was pushed over and sprained an ankle. He was not badly injured and actually walked back down unaided to Hayfield, but much was made of this in the subsequent trial. In passing, it is surprising who actually took part in the 1932 trespass. For example, the famous historian A.J.P. Taylor was there, as was the composer Michael Tippett, and I have already noted the participation of Ewan MacColl, who penned the outstanding song 'The Manchester Rambler' to put recall of the trespass forever into the back story of the fight for the right to roam.

Returning the way they had ascended, Benny and his group found the police waiting in numbers across the Kinder Road, and five of them were arrested. A sixth, John Anderson, aged twenty-one, had already been taken into custody and faced the most serious charge, one of grievous bodily harm for allegedly attacking the injured keeper. This charge was eventually changed to riot and assault, while Jud Clyne and Harry Mendel, both twenty-three, David Nussbaum and Tony Gillett, both nineteen, and Benny were charged with unlawful assembly and a breach of the peace.

Their subsequent trial in July 1932 before a jury at the Derby Assizes is I believe the reason that this became such a historic event: as well as resulting in major media coverage of the case, it highlighted the ongoing movement demanding public access to the countryside. Everything was legally unbalanced about the trial, which deserves the appellation of being truly a kangaroo court. Apart from a sprained ankle, no harm was done, but with the biased membership of the jury consisting of two brigadier generals, three colonels, two majors, three captains and two aldermen, even those in the outdoor world who had opposed the trespass became critical. And they were to be even more so when the sentences were handed down: six months for John Anderson, four months for Benny, two months each for Tony Gillett and Jud Clyne, and three months for David Nussbaum – one month of which was extra for selling the *Daily Worker*! Fortunately, Harry Mendel was discharged due to a lack of sufficient evidence to justify a conviction. The Manchester Ramblers' Federation approached the home secretary, requesting clemency, but were rebuffed by him. In any case, by that time the prisoners were well into their months of incarceration in Leicester jail.

While this was happening, on 26 June 1932 there was a massive turnout of approximately 10,000 people at a Winnats Pass demonstration, demanding 'free access to mountains'. It was addressed by Dr C.E.M. Joad, one of the best-known broadcasters and commentators of the period. This was followed in August by a protest rally at Jacob's Ladder on Kinder Scout at which the recently released Jud Clyne and other trespass supporters spoke out, demanding the right to roam. In September, a trespass north-west of Sheffield, at Abbey Brook, was of a different scale. On 16 October, however, an attempted trespass by ramblers and climbers at Stanage Edge was stopped in its tracks by mounted police and foot patrols with Alsatian dogs. But a flame had been lit, and in 1933 there was once again a large turnout at a Winnats Pass gathering, addressed by several leading politicians including Arthur Henderson. In the south of England, a thousand-strong demonstration demanding access was held at Leith Hill in Surrey; later, similar rallies took place in Wales and Scotland.

In 1931, the National Council of Ramblers' Federations had been formed, and the 1932 trespass seemed to concentrate their minds. The journalist Tom Criddle Stephenson, a major figure in that body and who became the secretary of the Ramblers' in 1948, was originally not a supporter of the Kinder trespass, but admitted, 'It had been the cockpit of the battle for the right to roam.' Praise indeed, for Stephenson held a unique position as a leading champion of walkers' rights in the countryside. Like Benny, he was from a working-class background, a true nonconformist, a pacifist who had been imprisoned in the First World War as a conscientious objector. He was, however, a man of vision who would subsequently inspire the creation of the Pennine Way and supported the setting up on 1 January 1935 of the Ramblers' Association – today simply called the Ramblers, a body which has over 100,000 members throughout the UK. Its credo is that rambling in the countryside is a right, and that it benefits the whole of British society. When I was at the BMC, we often found the Ramblers were ahead of the game when it came to access and conservation legalities, and they have always campaigned for full rights of responsible access to all of this country's open spaces. Stephenson was a tireless worker for these policies, a lead supporter of the need for national parks in order to conserve the most significant environmental areas of our country as well as a means to improve and guarantee access.

The demand for the setting up of national parks gathered pace throughout the late 1930s. In 1936, the first meeting of a body to investigate further the needs for such, the Standing Committee on National Parks, held an inaugural gathering, and in 1938 this resulted in a widely circulated and promoted paper by its secretary, John Dower, 'The Case for National Parks in Great Britain', which tipped the balance in favour of such: in 1939, an Access to Mountains Bill was finally passed by Parliament, but then the war intervened.

In 1945, the newly elected Labour government, under Prime Minister Clement Attlee, set up a new committee, chaired by a big hitter, Sir Arthur Hobhouse. It reported in 1947 and recommended that twelve national parks be set up as soon as legally and financially possible. I had by then started to climb and I can remember how, in such rambling and outdoor groups that one might meet at Ilkley, there was huge excitement about these proposals. But Yorkshire being Yorkshire, a mass demonstration was organised at the Cow and Calf demanding that the Yorkshire Dales be one of the first such parks to be set up. It was to be 1954 before this happened.

In 1949, after long and difficult negotiations in Parliament, the National Parks and access to the Countryside Act was finally passed into law. Guided there by Lewis Silkin, the minister of town and country planning, he declared, 'It is a people's charter – a people's charter for the open air.' In 1951, the first national park was set up in the Peak District. I think this was no accident, since it invoked Tom Stephenson's views on the Kinder Mass Trespass but expanded these to cover the whole of the Peak, the vanguard of the battle for a right of access. There are now fifteen national parks throughout the UK; the Lake District, Snowdonia and Dartmoor were also set up in 1951, inviting one to wonder if we will ever again experience another such reforming government as Attlee's.

I believe the 1949 Act was the most important in my lifetime. It did not magically open up all the prime climbing and walking sites, but it set in motion the belief that access was a right, generally supported by government on behalf of the whole population. Slowly, the barriers came down and, concentrating on the Peak, in 1955 the first access agreement for Kinder Scout was signed, followed in 1962 by a Stanage Edge agreement. In 1980, the Peak District National Park Authority purchased the Roaches estate, and so on. Maybe I have concentrated this access history too much on the bodies I know of and have worked with in the past, but many other individuals and organisations put their shoulders to the wheel to achieve the position we enjoy today, including the Open Spaces Society and groups such as SCAM, the Sheffield Campaign for Access to Moorland, as well as the Woodcraft Folk who were involved in supporting the Winnats Pass demonstrations. The Council for the Preservation of Rural England (CPRE) contributed to a voluntary warden system whenever it was felt it needed to buttress access. Many other persons were also involved.

In 1982, the National Trust acquired Kinder Scout. Benny Rothman was recruited as a voluntary advisor on recreational activities, and in 1990 the Rights of Way Act was established by a private members' bill. In 2000 came the Countryside and Rights of Way Act (CROW), and later the Land Reform (Scotland) Act 2003, both intended to improve access for the general public. Under the CROW Act, all rights of way, footpaths and open access in England and Wales must be recorded by 1 January 2026, while the rights confirmed in the Scottish Act are even greater than CROW due in part to the work of the late Alan Blackshaw.* The final piece in this complicated process is the Marine and Coastal Access Act 2009, concerned with access to coastal paths, beaches, sea cliffs and the like.

That is the story so far: on paper a successful outcome, but noting Benny Rothman's advice about how difficult it is to preserve such freedoms, it is germane to advise those now charged with preserving and improving our freedoms to be ever-vigilant on the climbing and rambling fraternities' behalf.

But what happened to Benny after the Kinder Mass Trespass? His was a life written large in radical action: battling against the British Union of Fascists in the 1930s, a trade unionist, a shop steward for the Amalgamated Engineering Union working on aircraft production during the war; this was to override his wish to join the services. Later, he advised and participated in many local and national organisations serving the wider community. In 1991, he presented a programme for Channel 4 about the history of the power held in the British landscape, who owned what and who had access to it, a subject still of great interest as I write, for in recent news is a finding that despite the (failed?) attempts to create a more equal society, more than fifty per cent of the land in this country is held by just one per cent of the population. Owning large tracts of land often leads on to great wealth, and many of the access agreements we enjoy today have come about by either considerable payments to landowners for agreeing to these, or by generous tax benefits.

In 1996, Benny was made an honorary life member of the Ramblers, and when he died in 2002, a blue plaque commemorating his life was placed at his former home in Timperley. In April 2007, the Ramblers celebrated the seventy-fifth anniversary of the Kinder Trespass and the imprisonment of five of those who participated, and many hundreds attended this televised gathering. Previously, on the fiftieth anniversary in April 1982, a commemorative plaque was placed in the quarry on the Kinder Road, which has now become a place of pilgrimage for those who realise the real meaning of the Kinder Mass Trespass, a truly significant event in the movement demanding public access to the countryside.

This article first appeared on *Footless Crow* in May 2019.

---

* Ed: the CROW Act deadline has since been extended to 1 January 2031.

15

LET THERE BE LIGHT

'At either moment let thy feet repair
  To Gordale chasm, terrific as the lair
  Where the young Lions couch'

— WORDSWORTH, FROM HIS SONNET, 'GORDALE'

It seems that all is fair in love, war and new routing, and historically there are many examples of mountaineers and rock climbers who have embraced this motto in their pioneering activities. One can think of several examples of such an approach: Ron Moseley on the first ascent of the *White Slab* of Clogwyn Du'r Arddu, Pete Crew on the *Central Pillar* of Esk Buttress, the race between British and French climbers for the Frêney Pillar of Mont Blanc, even the Swiss and British mountaineers on Mount Everest.

The only occasion in which I was involved in such a competitive act was for the first ascent of *Light* at Gordale Scar in the spring of 1964. This occurred on the cusp of the free climbing revolution on Yorkshire limestone; in the guidebook, *Light* is recorded as the first free major route in the gorge.

Gordale is a unique and impressive geological feature, rivalling both Malham Cove and Kilnsey Crag as the foremost climbing ground in the area. It lies at the end of the Craven Fault line, which runs from the borders of Cumbria into the Yorkshire Dales, and was formed 15–16 million years ago. Historically, Gordale Scar has been the inspiration for many works of art and literature, one of the earliest by the poet Thomas Gray who declared he could only bear to stay inside the gorge for fifteen minutes, and even that was 'not without shuddering'. But stouter hearts, the painters James Ward and J.M.W. Turner, both produced major studies of Gordale which can now be viewed at Tate Britain. Recently, the well-known local artist Ashley Jackson has produced several studies which I believe have captured the magical raw power of the gorge and its two impressive waterfalls.

To return to spring 1964: I was at the gorge accompanied by several fellow Rock and Ice members and we were searching out new route possibilities. I noted the impressive crack and groove lines seaming the buttress above the first waterfall, and I persuaded Terry Burnell to attempt these with me. In 1962, he had already pioneered two aid routes in the gorge, the *Ivy Groove* and *Rebel,* so he was well attuned to Gordale action, but my intention was to climb this new route as free as possible.

The route started at an obvious overhanging seven-metre crack just left of the arête above the waterfall. Leading, I found this to be beyond me to climb free, and so I managed to jam a sling in the crack and pull up on this. It transpired that the initial crack is actually the crux of the route and is now graded 5c. This fissure led into a niche, where I belayed, and Terry climbed up to join me. Taking over the lead, he climbed a short, cracked wall out on the left and then managed to traverse back right to gain the base of an impressive clean-cut corner groove. Jamming up this, he was stopped by a huge, loose block at its head. The obvious route from there was to traverse left under the capping roof, but just gingerly touching the rock which barred his progress made him realise that if it came away it would probably kill us both. With much shouting between us he retreated, down-climbing back to me, after which we abseiled off.

As it was now getting late on a Sunday afternoon, we decided we would return as soon as possible and abseil down the route to prise off the loose block in order to be able to complete the climb safely. I had named it 'Light' because it was next to the looming cave-type route nearby, known to us as 'Darkness', first climbed earlier that year by our friends John Midgley, Dick Watson and Tom Morrell.

The following weekend was a Rock and Ice Club meet in the Peak District and I was surprised to note that Dez Hadlum, one of my closest friends and fellow club members, was missing. This was unusual for him, as he faithfully attended such gatherings. I was stunned to learn later that he had recruited a fellow Nottingham-based climber, Eric Wallis, and they had then travelled up to Gordale, abseiled down *Light*, removed the huge loose block, after which Dez had led the route. This effort is now noted in the guidebook as one of the outstanding achievements in the history of Yorkshire climbing, and although like me they had needed to use aid on the first pitch, it is the brilliant twenty-eight-metre second pitch, now graded 5b, which makes the route a three-star E2 classic. This action of Dez's was totally out of character, for he was the last person one would have expected to be moved by such a competitive streak.

I had previously spent two long Alpine seasons with him during which we climbed over thirty routes together; he was the most equable partner imaginable. But he had watched Terry and me attempt *Light*, realised what a plum line it was, and new route fever had taken hold. However, once I got over my initial shock at this action, I had to admire his initiative, and we remained good friends.

Unfortunately, in 1969, there occurred on *Light* a terrible accident when the leader, Pete Callum, was killed because of belay failure. This was before the development of Friends, and subsequently a belay stake was placed in the banking above the route because prior to this placement it was difficult to find a suitable anchor point. The death of Pete was a terrible blow, for he was a well-known West Yorkshire activist, a member of the Yorkshire Mountaineering Club and a good friend. A song which always brings him to mind was current that year, number one in the hit parade in this country and in four others: 'Where Do You Go To (My Lovely)?' by Peter Sarstedt. We used to sing verses of this on occasion, parodying our own words – 'You climb like Tubby Austin, and jam like Joseph Brown' – at summer Wednesday evening gatherings on our local gritstone outcrops.

I always wanted to go back to *Light* and free climb the route, but it was to be many years before the gloom hanging over this route was dispelled after Pete's death. When I finally did return, on a midweek evening, it was with a climber from a younger generation, John Jefferies. We had by then modern protection equipment such as nuts and Friends and I managed to lead the initial crack free, while John led the second pitch in fine style without any alarms.

After the climb we retreated to the bar of the Buck Inn in Malham, and what happened there that night is one of those amazing coincidences of a kind you just cannot imagine. There were no other climbers in the bar, I guess because it was not the weekend, but there was a mixed group of walkers including a dark-haired guy who had a guitar at his side. After much persuasion he got up and started to play and sing, 'Where Do You Go To (My Lovely)?' He was outstandingly good, and as it is a song with such connotations for me, I felt when he had finished that I had to go over and congratulate him.

'Man, that was outstanding! You sang it as good as the original by Peter Sarstedt.'

He started to laugh out loud but then modestly informed me, 'I *am* Peter Sarstedt!'

Now, whenever I hear the strains of the accordion which open up the recording of that song, I think about *Light* and I am happy that my own initial attempt on that climb led on to the creation of one of the area's most classic routes.

This article first appeared in *Climber* in February 2016.

16

OLYMPIC DREAMS

'Citius, Altius, Fortius.'

— ORIGINAL MOTTO OF THE OLYMPIC GAMES

To represent a country at the Olympics is the ultimate dream of any games player and participant in athletic events. I am still in awe of the Czech athlete Emil Zátopek, who won the 5,000 metres, 10,000 metres and the marathon at the Games in Helsinki in 1952. I was privileged to meet him when young; his feat is unlikely ever to be repeated. I am a supporter of the Games, but I believe the inclusion of sport climbing at the recent Tokyo Olympics raises questions, at least with old timers like me.

The modern Olympic Games were brought about by the initiative of the French nobleman Baron de Coubertin, and the first of these was held in Athens in 1896. Mountaineering was one of the physical activities that he envisaged being recognised as an Olympic discipline: the members of the 1922 Everest expedition were awarded gold medals at the 1924 Winter Games, held in Chamonix. This continued until the Dyhrenfurths in 1936, awarded for their Himalayan explorations, but were then discontinued.

It is interesting to report how climbing was seen by commentators and artists up to almost modern times – let us be dog in a manger about this.

Ernest Hemingway opined that there are only three sports, 'bullfighting, flying and mountaineering; the rest are merely games'. I guess what brought him to such a view was that the sports he nominated were undertaken for keeps. The obituary section in the *Alpine Journal* at this time would illustrate where he was coming from.

In my own times, I have to ponder on the many who, having felt 'the romance of mountaineering', pushed the boat out, were caught out by a run of bad luck and paid the ultimate price. But we survivors paid our respects and kept alive their feats and memories. One of the salient facts being there was little or no money in it; recognition such as it was, came mainly from one's peers. I still think of how we all, in our milieu, greeted the news that Brown had climbed the *Boulder* on Cloggy. He had run out 270 feet of rope in a single lead, on sight, because none of his companions could follow him owing to the conditions. So how come that such a committing activity can be cut down to racing up an artificial wall, on plastic holds, safe because such 'climbing' is protected by bolts?

The 1972 Olympics in Munich was the first time that 'speed climbing' became a demonstration sport. This was on a limestone crag outside the city and by a group of climbers from Soviet Russia, wearing on their feet what appeared to us Western climbers who witnessed this to be galoshes. It transpired that the climbers had spent some days practising the route(s), and their ascents were at speed on top ropes. All who witnessed this – from many different nationalities – thought this style of climbing was rather pointless and preferred to climb the excellent traditional routes that were on offer at this cliff. One can understand a group of climbers moving quickly up routes in friendly rivalry, but to make this an Olympic sport is surely bringing such an activity down to a questionable level. And yet some of the non-climbing commentators thought this was like the Wacky Races; they conferred instant recognition and liking on some of the participants. I suppose it will go well when those involved are collared by agents and sponsors. And that is a problem for those so involved: are they to declare that this really has nothing to do with 'real' climbing or do they milk this surprising turn of events?

For the first time, real amounts of money are involved when one is apprised by UK Sport that one of the Olympic programmes of the national sports bodies was underwritten by £27 million. And for any of those who might win a medal, their day-to-day living is being underwritten, as are their coaches, medics and dieticians. It is estimated that each gold medal costs around £1 million. The athletes involved can, if they wish, become full-time professionals. Such designation leads on to sponsorships, deals with equipment firms and large amounts of money changing hands.

A worry is how this came about without the traditional defenders of the British way of climbing not really taking an interest. Their attitude is that if a group within the mountain world wishes to do this, 'let 'em get on with it,' without at least discussing how in the long run it might affect the activity, which as recently as the 1980s was a new kid on the international climbing scene.

At the BMC in 1988, we came to accepting organised competitions after months of argument and discussions, but we were only willing to accept them as long as they were held on artificial walls and not on the natural outcrops and crags. This decision was influenced by what was happening on the natural cliffs. Ron Fawcett was despatched to competitions held in Russia and reported that many of the routes involved in these were chipped and manufactured. Visiting Czechoslovakian climbers who had taken part that year in competitions held in Arco reported that the final route of the event was similarly prepared specially for that competition.

Despite the above, what finally swung the then British climbing fraternity behind supporting competitions, but only on artificial walls, was the attempt to hold a major competition at Malham. Those involved were leading climbers of the era, and the BBC were interested in covering the event, despite this being in opposition to the wishes of the locals, the RSPB and the national park.

The view we came to at the BMC was that this could damage climbing in the future. I was tasked with contacting all concerned and using what arguments we could muster against such a badly thought-out initiative. We pointed out that if it rained and conditions changed, the whole competition could become unfair and farcical, to say nothing of the safety of the inevitable spectators roaming around an area like the Cove. We had to go almost to the top of the BBC to head off the interest in covering the event. Fortunately, our arguments were soundly based and eventually all came round to the opinion that competitions should be held in the UK only on artificial walls. Since then, the growth of competition climbing and climbing walls has been impressive, with over 400 noted in the last complete survey. Many bouldering competitions are run in the winter; the Leeds Wall did that when I was the chair of its board.

We never expected it, but it is now a fact, that some of the attendees at climbing walls never climb outside, and for personal reasons have no wish to do so. If I was still an active climber, selfishly I would declare, 'good on 'em!' for it would mean less traffic on popular crags. Frankly, though, they do not know what they are missing, a special activity that is life enhancing: going to the hills to refresh one's soul. Easily dismissed as romantic gibberish, but it is true as those who experience such feelings bear witness.

International competition climbing became a fact in Leeds in 1989 at the first world cup. This was organised by the BMC and DMM, the equipment firm, on behalf of the then recognised body for such an international event, the UIAA. It took place in Leeds because that is where I lived. Friends interceded for us, and we managed to obtain the Queen's Hall, which previously had staged massive rock concerts: the Rolling Stones, the Beatles and The Who had strutted their stuff on its stage. The women's event was won by the American Robyn Erbesfield, and the men's by Jerry Moffatt. It was very much a learning event for such a competition, and it made me think that while the finals were electrifying, the events leading up to them were so boring that I could never believe it a spectator sport. In fact, one of the sports journalists collared me after some of the preliminary rounds to declare he was departing: 'This is like watching paint dry.' I could understand this, as the majority of the participants did not get very far up the routes. It is a mystery to me that climbers can sit and watch such a competition while close by, at Arco, for instance, excellent climbing is offered on natural rock. But as Cyndi Lauper warned us, 'money changes everything,' and I suppose there is a vicarious pleasure in watching the winner and losers.

Finally, my reaction to Olympic climbing is ditch the speed competition: it is a cuckoo, and not only has it no place in such a context, in the long run it may damage the sport. Non-climbers will think that is how we proceed on the natural crags and outcrops and the land managers may react in ways that no one has yet experienced. The walls should be designed like crags to be more realistic. I have been lucky to climb at such in dozens of countries and have never found features like those that were a part of the Olympic bouldering competition. Dalí would have been exercised by their design. I am very aware that by expressing such views I will be the subject of criticism and gales of laughter. The wish to compete is part of the psyche in a lot of humans, and we must accept that climbing is changing and a part of mainstream sport, no longer the preserve of a band of clubbable types. But we have to point out what is worth preserving, that the rock faces and mountains of this world we expect will always be there, posing a challenge and offering enjoyment to those who answer their call.

This article first appeared on *Footless Crow* in December 2021.

REVIEWS

17

UNKNOWN PLEASURES
BY ANDY KIRKPATRICK

Andy Kirkpatrick. © Kirkpatrick Collection

Andy Kirkpatrick grew up in straitened circumstances on a council estate in Hull and for many years he has been doing his own thing, almost a *Loneliness of the Long Distance Runner*, seeking out climbs where the danger is real and safety questionable, confounding his critics and delighting audiences with his stand-up comedy performances based on his life and hard times on some of the gnarly big walls and mountain faces of the world.

Having noted this, I expected *Unknown Pleasures* – the title gleaned from a Joy Division album – to be a laugh a minute, albeit couched in fruity discourse; but no, I found this a serious and thought-provoking read. I only laughed out loud once while digesting its contents.

There must be something in the water in Hull and its surroundings, for besides this author, Joe Tasker, John Redhead and Alex MacIntyre all hailed from its flat landscapes. It is interesting, however, to think on this author's family name, not Yorkshire at all, but lowland Scots. We are such a mixture in this country, but this Kirkpatrick is I guess almost a one-off. Despite him being seriously dyslexic, undiagnosed until his late teens – he admits he cannot spell or punctuate, nor has he any grammatical ability – he has twice won the Boardman Tasker Prize for Mountain Literature.

In my opinion, his first winner, *Psychovertical,* is a modern classic about climbing and climbers. *Unknown Pleasures* is a collection of thirty-two essays, the range of subjects covered best described as 'diverse'. So much so that I had to stop reading on occasion to reassess my own thoughts on some of the topics included. Yes, there are some essays that are about hardcore climbing, but others that touch on relationships, parenting, mental health including suicide, the workings of the media and its misuse, abortion, Nazi atrocities in a French village in the Second World War and so much more. I do not think it will be 'big' with those who get their kicks from climbing only indoors on plastic, but if you wish to be made to think about the meaning of it all then this might be the book for you.

The trolls, however, are already at work on so-called social media, which is not social at all, and often uninformed, but I think the author is of such a background that he can turn their ill-thought-out criticisms to his own advantage. Maybe we should note here his thirty-plus ascents of El Capitan, five of which have been solo, including his ascent of the *Reticent Wall* which was the central theme of *Psychovertical*, his ski crossing of Greenland, and climbs in Patagonia, Alaska and Antarctica, as well as his writings about these adventures. These now seem to have enabled him to write and unburden himself about events and relationships that have troubled him in his past.

Each essay is illustrated with one of his line drawings. Some, like his drawing of a fox's face, are outstanding, though the drawing of a frog is a little less so. But each piece of artwork must have required much thought and preparation; in many instances, they add a lot to the overall feel of the work.

The essays are gathered into five themes, each with a heading to set the scene. The first, 'Climbing, Expeditions and Adventures', includes twelve pieces; the second 'Looking On', four, and so on. Between three of these we are treated to 'Bad Poetry' – 'The Mountain', 'Winter' and 'POLY WALL'. It is hard for me to suggest whether these are good or bad, for poems are so personal and often mean something to their composer that the reader finds difficult to comprehend. The essays carry so much feeling that at times I found myself wondering why the author had decided to let us in on the trials and tribulations within his personal relationships. I cannot think of any other climber who has done this with such honesty.

The climbing essays are as one would expect from this writer: page turners. Those about his early life in Hull, 'The Land of Green Ginger' and 'High Marks', when he was finally diagnosed with extreme dyslexia, are interesting, and in the case of the latter, educative. What undiagnosed problem might we also be suffering from? I was always unbelieving when Don Whillans confessed that he suffered from an undiagnosed vertigo condition, but having read Kirkpatrick's story, maybe we were unsympathetic to the Villain's plight in that respect?

The two climbing essays I enjoyed the most were 'The Troll's Gift' and 'Queen Maud Land', the first about attempts and a successful ascent of the Troll Wall in Norway, and the second about being some kind of guide to a party of Norwegians intent on climbing Ulvetanna, a difficult mountain which they wished to ascend then base jump from its summit. In setting the scene for this adventure, he decides that he must start thinking about the cold conditions like his companions. They seem totally inured to such. I can vouchsafe for this, when one winter in the 1980s in Lappland I made a winter climb with a Swede and two Norwegians. The latter spent each winter weekend camping near some climbing objective; their secret in combating the freezing conditions, they informed me, was by sleeping on reindeer skin mats. I think the author's writing in this essay is among his finest and, despite his Norwegian partners on this climb being novices, they were successful in climbing a mountain which had previously been regarded as extremely difficult.

This is a surprising fact about some of Kirkpatrick's climbs: he climbed the *Nose* route on El Capitan with a scratch team of Irish climbers –

including his second wife – some of whom had never multi-pitched previously; another stand-out adventure was an ascent of El Capitan with his thirteen-year-old daughter Ella. As someone who was in the Valley in 1966 and can still recall the awe that such routes were held in at that time, I can only gasp in admiration at his chutzpah! Warren Harding, however, the pioneer of the *Nose* route over many days of effort, would in my experience – as I knew him quite well and actually climbed with him on Yorkshire gritstone – no doubt now be falling about laughing at the 'downward bound' standing of his climbs in the Yosemite Valley, including the *Dawn Wall*.

One essay, 'Celebrity Abuse', that I am sure will be read with interest, describes the ascent of the Moonlight Buttress in Zion National Park with Alex Jones, presenter of the BBC's *The One Show*, for all such live TV presentations have the potential for spinning out of control. The author had no idea who Alex Jones was when he was asked to lead this event, mistaking the name for Aled Jones, the former choirboy! Only one training session was completed at the Castle Climbing Centre in London, where poor Miss Jones, who was not a climber, was taught how to tie in, prussik and move up and down the wall. Despite all the difficulties the climb was successful, although we learn from the essay that several juicy bits were cut from the broadcast. It was well received and raised over £1 million for Sport Relief.

One matter which the author does not avoid in his big-walling stories is the business of toileting. One can imagine that Alex Jones must have found it off-putting for such a non-climber and media star to be on this wall in Utah and be expected to poo into a paper bag.

The later essays do take on ever more serious themes, especially those under the heading 'Life, Death and In Between'. The death of Dean Potter, in the essay 'The Artist', affected the author deeply for he was by any standards an amazing adventurer: climber, base jumper, slack liner and a Yosemite legend, but, true to his Yorkshire roots, Kirkpatrick does not endorse empty eulogising, just remembering the meet-ups, the banter and the friendly support from such an outstanding personality. Nor has he any wish to be involved in climbing circuses like those now surrounding TV personalities or Everest junkets, hitting home hard and true with his views in 'Everest Sucking on the Barrel'.

His final essays, which he classifies as 'Unidentifiable', have little to do with climbing and much to do with life, in all its different forms. The essay

'Roger Godfrin' is disturbing, for it deals with a terrible massacre in a French village, Oradour-sur-Glane, by men of the Waffen-SS. Roger Godfrin was a young boy who disobeyed the orders to line up, and who said to a friend, 'They're Germans, they will hurt us. I'm going to try and escape.' And he did, while the hundreds who obeyed orders from their teachers, priests and the SS were all murdered.

The book finishes with an epilogue, 'What I've Learned', where in 'Not Your Man' you get the essence of what Kirkpatrick is about. He is not a made-over, Instagram warrior. He certainly tries to tell it without flim-flam as it appears to him: for instance, although now living in Ireland with his second wife, who is from that country, he is not afraid to give us his views on abortion. In another judgement piece he lets rip about the CIA, the Contras, Nicaragua, drugs and the secret Iran arms deal, and much more. He also tells us that a gay contact had told him that if he also was such, he would be a 'bear'.* His wife likes to refer to him as 'Polar Bear' for he is physically solidly built! Typical of his roots in the East Riding is that he is an avid tea drinker.

So, I leave it at that, a most unusual book from a talented writer. I guess it is not going too far to declare him an artist. I have no doubt that some will find this book controversial, demanding and challenging. But I enjoyed reading it and would recommend others to do the same. It is well produced as a casebound book that meets the high standards Vertebrate have set for this type of production.

Andy Kirkpatrick, *Unknown Pleasures* (Sheffield: Vertebrate Publishing, 2018).

This review first appeared on *Footless Crow* in February 2018.

---

* Bear: slang for a gay man of rugged appearance and personality.

18

MASTERMIND BY JERRY MOFFATT

'Man knows much more than he understands.'

— ALFRED ADLER

This is the third book published by the Café Kraft organisation covering training systems for climbing. Who are Café Kraft in this instance? An organisation based in Germany, with ultra-modern climbing centres in Nuremberg and Stuttgart, at the cutting edge of where training for sport climbing and bouldering is developing. Looming over their story are the progenitors of redpoint, Norbert Sander and Kurt Albert, and the figure of the late Wolfgang Güllich, who, despite being the tragic victim of a car crash in 1992, was one of the first of the 'modern' elite to bring scientific training methods into his development as a climber. A sports physiology student at Erlangen university, studying under the famous Professor Dr Weineck, Wolfgang applied his knowledge to his climbing and set new standards for sport climbing with routes like *Action Directe* (F9a) in the Frankenjura, Germany, and *Punks in the Gym* (F8b+) in Arapiles, Australia. Also noteworthy are some outstanding alpine rock climbs, such as *Riders on the Storm* on the Central Tower of Paine in Patagonia, climbed with fellow Germans Kurt Albert, Bernd Arnold, Norbert Bätz and Peter Dittrich.

Jerry Moffatt. © Moffatt Collection

Jerry Moffatt came into the spotlight of British climbing in the early 1980s. For the next two decades, he roamed far and wide, pioneering high-standard new routes and boulder problems, participating in competitions, and making early repeats in countries as diverse as Britain, France, Germany, the USA, Japan and Australia. Learning from these experiences and agreeing with Güllich that, 'The mind is the most important muscle,' he has set down in *Mastermind* what he believes are the most important elements in mental training for climbers, guided by two climbers with relevant professional backgrounds: Professor Lew Hardy from Bangor University, and Dr Noel Craine, an epidemiology researcher in the NHS. This knowledge is formulated in short chapters covering such subjects as visualisation, motivation, goal setting and planning, rehearsal, as well as conscious and unconscious thought. The book's layout and setting are truly modern and are typical of the author, a 'with it' mindset bolstered by wise sayings and epigrams: everyone from Muhammad Ali and Lao Tzu to Bruce Lee. Unfortunately, there are a number of spelling and grammatical errors in the text, but they do not affect one's understanding of any meaning of the contents.*

The mass of climbers who do not aim to be part of an elite performance programme, who climb only for their own enjoyment and 'fun', may ask, 'Why should I bother?' Well, exploration of the mind is not time wasted, and may be helpful in facing up to life's inevitable problems in other spheres of our existence. Present-day research into this still rests heavily on the work of three men at the end of the nineteenth and early part of the twentieth centuries: Sigmund Freud, Carl Jung and Alfred Adler. Each developed their own take on this subject, but the fact of all humans possessing a conscious and unconscious mind is paramount to the understanding of our behaviour.

Inevitably, as psychology has developed and new discoveries have been made, there has grown a plethora of specialisations: educational psychology, social psychology, child psychology, clinical psychology and so on, but the one of most interest to climbing is sports psychology. The core disciplines of performance are biomechanics, kinesiology, physiology and psychology, and within climbing's disciplines of sport, boulder and competition, climbers are coming to appreciate the importance of psychology. I guess they are the climbers that Moffatt's book is now aimed at. This is bolstered by a quote elsewhere by Shauna Coxsey, a two-time bouldering world cup champion and the only British climber to qualify for the Tokyo Olympics: 'I long ago came to realise in this sport, psychology is way more important than physiology!'

To return to *Mastermind*: we learn the thoughts and ambitions of several of today's leading boulder, sport and competition climbers, including Margo Hayes, Adam Ondra, Alex Megos and Chris Sharma, and from Jerry himself. Winning in Leeds in 1989 at the first world cup competition was a major achievement in his life. This is also a matter of pride for me, for I was heavily involved in organising this along with DMM, and the competition took place in Leeds where I live. Friends of mine owned the venue and I persuaded them to let us use their main hall. But *Mastermind* is not just about those involved in what many see as the modern disciplines in climbing, for also included with their ideas and thoughts about mind control are Leo Houlding, Sandy Allan, Pete Whittaker, Stefan Glowacz, Jimmy Webb, Alex Honnold and many more, covering everything from an epic ascent in

---

* Ed: subsequently corrected in the 2022 Vertebrate edition.

the Himalaya, base and wing suit flying, bouldering, and a twenty-four-hour ascent of El Capitan. One interview that really gripped was that with Mich Kemeter, using a breathing technique and slackline walking between two balloons set at 1,000 metres up in the sky. Many of these events are included as inspirational stories at the end of the book. However, talking about the use of a breathing technique to keep the level of anxiety or fear at managed levels in order to undertake a dangerous challenge like slackline walking, I have to observe that this is nothing new.

It is obvious that Jerry is as impressed with Chinese martial artists as I am. They are masters at such techniques which are common practice in some of their meditations. I have visited the Shaolin Si in Henan, China, on two occasions: the monks there have developed gong (kung) fu techniques for over a thousand years. Unfortunately, they have become a part of the entertainment industry – and maybe that is what competition climbing will also develop into given time – but they can still perform some amazing feats. Also, when in Jiangyou in Sichuan, China, I witnessed a Daoist monk perform a staggering feat, a one-finger handstand. On another occasion in northern Sichuan, I observed a monk tightrope walking between two high rock pinnacles. He had no safety line and if he had fallen it would have been terminal. Finally, in reporting the observation of Chinese mind-training activities, adherents following t'ai chi exercises can be observed anywhere in parks throughout China. The one activity I have seriously studied was at a qigong centre on the isle of Hainan off the south coast of the mainland; it was most rewarding. In this, one follows a strict regime of exercises, calligraphy, meditation and so on. Learning how to harness the power of one's centre using qi is both relaxing and impressive. It is why a qigong master who came to the UK sat down and challenged a group of Royal Marines to lift him. They could not, and interesting for Jerry's benefit might be the information that Bruce Lee of *Enter the Dragon* fame was taught by such a master.

Humans have known for generations about the potential for harnessing the power of the mind, and though slow to accept sports psychology in Britain, it was adopted much earlier in the USA. Coleman Griffith of the University of Illinois is credited as one of the founders of this discipline. In 1918, he began to use cognitive and behavioural strategies to improve the performance of basketball and American football team members; in 1925, he opened the first research laboratory in psychology and its relation to athletic performance. In the mid-1980s, I was invited to join the board of the association of British sports psychologists. At that time, we still lagged far behind Germany, led by Dr Carl Diem in Berlin, who, like the USA, had adopted the discipline as early as 1925. We in the UK had hardly noted the fact that 450 sports psychologists from many countries had gathered in Rome in 1965 for the discipline's first world congress. An amusing anecdote occurred when one of my fellow board members was invited by the manager of one of the First Division soccer clubs in 1986 to advise his players and to help them begin adopting psychometric methods in their training. He came back, chastened, for the team had ganged up on him and refused to take part in any mind training. They totally misunderstood what he was about and felt it was a dark suggestion that some of them were mentally unstable. Remember that the First Division became the Premier League just a few years later, so this was an indication of how far behind they were in adopting what are now the accepted norms in such training.

Sports psychology came of age at the Olympics in 1984, and at the 1996 Summer Olympics, the USA athletics team had a group of twenty psychologists accompanying their participants. It is now the norm for sports psychologists to be a part of our elite and national teams, including even the Premier League football clubs.

I am sure, like me, Jerry Moffatt sees climbing as a different kind of sport from athletics, although the latter is a sport in which I have also been involved. He started climbing as a fifteen-year-old and was prepared to 'rough it' just to get out on to the crags. I started as an eleven-year-old, and used to walk long distances to do the same at a time when our country was still recovering from the Second World War. I would have suggested to him when he was putting together *Mastermind* to give an indication of where he thought climbing was travelling to. It is still a broad church, with boulder, trad, sport, competition, alpine and greater ranges mountaineering all a part of climbing. But will it remain so with Olympic recognition? From what I have experienced, although several times in *Mastermind* we learn that training and competing is all about having 'fun', it does seem awfully serious now, with little or no hint that anarchy might still break out, given half a chance to do so. As I have observed before, 'Quo vadis, climbing?'

Finally, the book is illustrated with many fine photographs and is intended to be used as a training manual. At the end of some of the subsections there are lined pages to write thoughts and detail as in a diary of where the climber is at in their training methods and progress, for example, in 'Strength'. Into the case binding is bound a page marker and a pencil holder. I am informed that *Mastermind* has sold 12,000 copies outside the UK, so it will be interesting to note how it is received here. Doubtless it will be like its author: another milestone in our own climbing story.

Jerry Moffatt, *Mastermind* (Nuremberg: Café Kraft, 2019; Sheffield: Vertebrate Publishing, 2022).

This review first appeared on *Footless Crow* in December 2019.

19

CRAZY SORROW: THE LIFE
AND DEATH OF ALAN MULLIN

'No price is too high to pay for the privilege of owning yourself.'

— RUDYARD KIPLING

I faced the thought of reading *Crazy Sorrow* with some trepidation, for I already knew Alan Mullin's climbing story, and had read Ed Douglas's article in the *Guardian* about his terrible death. I feared that in learning about what had led up to that, some of my own father's mental breakdown would be in my recall, although unlike Alan Mullin, my sister and I never suffered physical abuse at home.

The story begins with a short foreword by his brother Kevin, three years younger than Alan. Like Alan, he also joined the army, finishing as a senior NCO. There then follows an authoritative overview, 'The Discipline of Suffering', by the historical guru of Scottish winter climbing Simon Richardson. This covers the earliest ascent of Ben Nevis to collect plant specimens in 1771, to a winter climbing grade X,10 and beyond 200 years later. All the major historical figures and their climbs are included; the story finishes around the time Alan Mullin begins his ascents, moving up unbelievably in two years to the top of the grading system. Richardson explains how the system and its workings developed over so many winter seasons of trial and error. Being a pedant, I found only one mistake in this excellent review, on page 20: the first ascent of the north face of the Droites in September 1955 was made by P. Cornuau and M. Davaille.

A major part of the book details where Alan Mullin came from and how he grew up, beginning with his life in two different housing estates near Glasgow. His father was partly deaf, earned a living as a pipe fitter, but abandoned his family when Alan was thirteen, leaving him to fend for himself and his younger brother, with a mother who sank deeper and deeper into alcoholism while living off benefits, resulting in Kevin being removed into care. It is warts and all, for his father was a Protestant, and his mother a Catholic, and once his father had departed, Alan was moved from a Protestant school to a Catholic one. He became a Celtic supporter and on one occasion actually attended an Old Firm (Celtic versus Rangers) derby. This was at the latter's ground. Wearing his Celtic shirt, he was lucky to get away without a beating, for having lost a friend and transport home he was accosted by older, bigger Rangers fans who were ready for a fight, having lost the game to their Catholic rivals. He had the sense to get his shirt off and hide it from sight. For the uninitiated, the Protestant versus Catholic rivalry between these clubs' supporters has in the past been the cause of much violence.

In the early chapters, there is also violence and much fighting: Mullin had to learn the hard way that he needed to toughen up and assume the role of 'the hardest kid on our street'. And although he was physically small, he made up for this when challenged by his level of aggression. Unless you have experienced this kind of milieu yourself it may seem pointless, but we are a product of our environment, and if you live in any such area anywhere in the UK, it is likely you too might have experienced such a culture.

How do these sink estates develop? When I was fifteen, in 1951, I had met in Wales Mick Noon of Glasgow's Creagh Dhu Club (Mick is mentioned in Richardson's review); he had invited me to visit him and attend a club meet on the Cobbler. I hitch-hiked from Leeds and was met by Mick, who lived in the Gorbals, a sea of run-down tenements and dilapidated saloon bars. It is from the redevelopment of such inner-city areas into estates and new towns on the peripheries of major conurbations, with many of their denizens moving there from these districts, that some sink estates seem to develop. It is a national disgrace that in some of these places, levels of poverty and depression exist that no country should allow.

But let me be clear here: there was nothing depressed about the members of the Creagh Dhu when I eventually met up with them. As I was to find out, however, later in the mid-1960s while working for a firm in the Anderston district of Glasgow, many of these places on the fringe of the city were just as Alan Mullin experienced when young, districts to avoid unless you were also willing to trade a Glasgow kiss or two!

Mullin was determined to get himself out of his troubled environment, and as soon as he was able, at fifteen, he joined the army. Incredibly, he joined an English infantry regiment, the Green Jackets. After one year of basic training as a junior soldier, he was posted into the regiment's second battalion. Having expected life to be so different in the army, he quickly learned that it could be just as violent as it had been at school and on the two council estates on which he had lived. In another life, when I was forced into national service before I was posted to Manchester in February 1954, I had to undertake three weeks of infantry training in Wiltshire. This educated me on how such an existence can dehumanise anyone who is of a sensitive nature, for on one of those weeks I shared barracks with a young Jewish teenager who just could not stand the constant verbal attacks on him by the NCOs and the antagonism from bigoted fellow recruits, so he killed himself. In true army style, the ranks closed and though his parents, along with their MP, arrived at the camp demanding answers, the true situation as to what had happened was brushed aside without any real consideration by the officer corps.

I think I need here to give an insight into how such training affected Mullin: 'After almost a year of training, I had transformed from a scrawny young recruit into a finely tuned psycho with a thirst for violence: exactly what the army was looking for.'

Over the next eight years, Mullin served first in Northern Ireland at the height of the Troubles, then in Cyprus and finally in South Georgia. Good and bad things happened to him during these years. A positive one was meeting his wife Marion, whose first husband had also been in the military but who had died in a helicopter crash. But a negative one occurred when nearing the end of his tour in Northern Ireland, while engaged in the rumble of a game of indoor football, riflemen versus NCOs, he was rammed into a wall, badly fracturing a knee. This was so serious he was flown to the Woolwich military hospital in London, resulting in an operation and a month in bed before returning to Belfast. His final posting in

South Georgia perforce, because of the terrain, meant a course in mountain training, including some ice climbing. This is when he became fired up by the wish to become a climber.

Unfortunately, while on another exercise, carrying a heavy rucksack, he suffered a slipped disc which made continuing with this outing a physical agony. It was a big mistake to go on battling this, for he was doing himself real physical damage. I also once slipped a disc and was likewise in physical agony, but I had this dealt with within forty-eight hours by a neurosurgeon. It took me a few months to recover completely. Despite moving on to light duties, Mullin's situation became ever more serious and eventually resulted in him needing a spinal operation. This led to him being discharged from the service, a decision which he found hard to contemplate for, despite all else, he loved the army and had no wish to leave a life which he found so conducive to his own attitude to living. By the end of his story, I had to agree with a view expressed by his brother, that retiring him from the army on the grounds of physical disability was truly a questionable action.

On returning to civilian life, Alan moved with his family – his wife Marion had two children from her first marriage, and they had a son together – to a village near Invergordon, and for a time they seemed settled. However, Mullin was drinking heavily, on occasion experimenting with drugs and getting into fights in clubs (he acted as a bouncer for a short period), and he unfortunately found that life in what they had thought could be a honeyed existence in a traditional Highland village turned out not to be so. The result was a confrontation with a family of local troublemakers which ended with criminal charges in court, from which Mullin and his wife were completely exonerated. They then moved twenty miles away to another village, where they did find the lifestyle that they had originally sought, with an environment in which their three children could safely grow up. However, his heavy drinking, his drug taking, and bouts of anger and worries about where he was heading – he had been only twenty-three when he left the army – made him begin to question his mindset. He booked himself into a series of appointments with a psychologist and confessed that despite his apprehension about doing this, he found the meetings worthwhile and even enjoyable.

He then almost by accident rediscovered what he was good at: climbing. In the 1990s, mixed winter climbing was taking off, and after what was an unbelievably short apprenticeship of two years, he went from soloing at grade I to climbing at grade VIII. For Mullin, the hardships that go hand in hand with Scottish winter climbing seemed no worse than those he had come to expect in the army. Initially, he was very much self-motivated and self-taught, but in 1997 he teamed up with Steve Paget, a highly talented but relatively unknown winter climber. Together they focused predominantly on mixed climbs in the Cairngorms.

Making full use of the equipment revolution then under way, and the new technique of dry tooling, over the next few years, either partnered by Steve or climbing solo, Mullin repeated many classic Cairngorm mixed climbs. Simon Richardson notes that he was rapidly moving to the forefront of Scottish winter climbing. Ascent followed ascent, a standout climb being the *Needle* on the Shelter Stone Crag in a seventeen-hour push in 1998: a ten-pitch route, the first to be graded IX. They bettered this the following winter with an ascent of the *Steeple*, also on the Shelter Stone, seen by many at that time as the last great Scottish winter problem. Again, Simon Richardson opines that this ascent was, 'without question the most sustained technical winter route climbed in Scotland to date.'

Others were not so complimentary, however, for both these climbs were made early in the season, in the case of the *Needle* in late October, and I know from when I lived in Scotland it was rare that routes were in winter condition so early in the season. Conditions in an area like the Cairngorms change so much from year to year, and even from day to day. Not all the responses to these ascents, however, were critical. Andy Kirkpatrick noted, 'Alan was a revolutionary in the history of Scottish climbing, a total outsider who shook a closed scene to pieces.'

Alan further upped the ante by making an incredible on-sight solo first winter ascent of *Rolling Thunder* (VIII,8) on Lochnagar in December 1999. In summer conditions this is a four-pitch E1 5b. There was no doubt about the cliff being in winter condition on this occasion, for other climbers were in the area and took pictures with long lenses of the face on which Mullin appears as a red dot in a hanging sea of white.

One chapter I really enjoyed reading was about Mullin attending the 1999 BMC International Winter Climbing Meet based at Glenmore Lodge. As the person who organised the very first BMC international meet in Wales, in 1973, it was interesting to note how much had changed. I do not remember any of the attendees then being prima donnas, although some of the fifty-one climbers from nineteen countries had made major first ascents in their own countries and the Himalaya. It seemed that by 1999 some of those who were in attendance were such, and one of them in particular did not rate high on the Mullin personal behaviour acceptance scale. Good came from this, however, for Mullin met Kevin Thaw and Leo Houlding, with whom he did gel: before the meet was over, he had an invitation from Thaw to climb in the USA and Patagonia.

During 1999 and 2000, Mullin's desire to widen his experience led him to the USA, the Dolomites and Patagonia. In Yosemite, he completed his first ever big wall climb and aid route, the *Prow*. His first trip to Patagonia between January and March 2000 with Kevin Thaw, an expat Brit based in California, was very successful: the pair made a free ascent of the *Czech Route* (VI, 5.11) on Fitz Roy's west face, retreating just short of the summit. This was Alan's first of three trips to Patagonia; the other two were to be attempts on the infamous Maestri–Egger line on Cerro Torre. The first of these attempts, climbing again with Thaw but also accompanied by Leo Houlding, ended when the latter took a leader fall, badly fracturing an ankle, and the second attempt was totally bombed out by constant bad weather. At least some good came out of these last two trips, because Mullin made friends with the Austrian climber Peter Janschek and visited him for some ice climbing, of which there is plenty in that country. The famous photographer Heinz Zak, a friend of Peter's, accompanied them, resulting in an impressive picture in *Crazy Sorrow* of Alan leading an iced-up route at the *Rudolfshütte* winter ski and climbing area.

Back in Scotland in winter, first ascents and difficult repeats continued: *Centurion* (VIII,8) solo on Ben Nevis, the *Demon Direct* (IX,9) in the Northern Corries with Steve Paget, and *Crazy Sorrow* (IX,10) on Lochnagar with Steve Lynch. Over this latter climb – the first so highly graded as they proposed a grade of X,11 – a storm of criticism erupted. 'Pre-placed gear', 'abseil inspection', 'aided moves' and so on being the screams from the keyboard warriors, but also some of the protectors of the Scottish winter climbing ethic. Mullin either did not care or pretended not to. An innocent enquiry about this controversy from Simon Richardson hit a raw nerve and resulted in an unfriendly response to be followed by three abusive emails. And that was the last time Simon communicated with him, although he writes that despite everything he still regards Alan as a friend, and that he was the best winter climber of his day. Interestingly, Dave MacLeod, who also climbed with Mullin, gives him the same high rating but noted, 'He was without a doubt the most intense person I've ever spent time with or climbed with.' For those interested, the name *Crazy Sorrow* comes from a lyric in 'Mr Tambourine Man' by Bob Dylan, but it is also a book title by Susan Bowes about a deadly family feud in the Appalachian Mountains.

In 2004, Mullin abruptly announced he was giving up climbing: the injuries suffered during his army career had caught up with him. He had a knee operation in a private clinic in Sheffield in 2003, but he had to accept that his injured knee was ruined. He also still suffered from his spinal injury, for which he had continued to take an opioid pain killer.

Stopping climbing, in which his star had shone so brightly despite it being for such a brief period, seemed, as Kevin Thaw writes, 'the beginning of a downward spiral'. Marion noted, 'he became very withdrawn and we could see a dramatic change in him'. He was admitted twice in 2004 on an informal basis to the local psychiatric hospital in Inverness, and he was diagnosed with 'bipolar affective disorder – manic phase, personality disorder and possibly drug induced problems'.

He then became an outpatient, but in August 2005 failed to attend an appointment and thereafter had no contact with the hospital until his next admission in 2007. He had stopped taking the antipsychotic medications he had been prescribed, citing bad side effects. He tried to find new directions away from climbing by studying philosophy and psychology through the Open University. He was very enamoured of the writings of Nietzsche. He trained as an alcohol counsellor, but quickly gave that up, later enrolling on an anthropology course at the University of Aberdeen.

The whole terrible story then unfolds, and no one is better qualified to give insight into its development and causes than Grant Farquhar, the book's editor, for he is a practising psychiatrist. I will leave the reader to follow this to what may seem an inevitable demise, with Alan first attempting suicide by slashing his wrists, and then walking in front of a car on the A9, suffering an ankle fracture, damaged ribs and multiple soft tissue injuries. He spent eleven days in Raigmore Hospital in Inverness before being admitted to the care of his wife as a voluntary patient at the New Craigs psychiatric hospital.

Ten days after admission, the medical staff wanted him to stay, but he wished to go home. He discharged himself 'against medical advice', although once again he was prescribed a suitable antipsychotic medication. There was much more suffering for the family and Alan before the final breakdown, when he became so delusional his wife drove to the Dingwall police station to seek help. Two police officers followed her back to her house and managed to enter, but Alan told them to leave then moved himself upstairs to a bedroom, warning the policemen that to come up to him would be at their own peril. Knowing he had been in the army and was a trained combatant the police then called for backup. Fifteen officers arrived at the house, five in riot gear, along with negotiators and dogs.

Eventually, after five hours of stand-off and with Alan threatening, under orders of the area commander they removed him from the house. Instead of having him sectioned and admitted into hospital, due to multiple misunderstandings he was held in police cells and appeared the next day at Tain sheriff court charged with a breach of the peace. Rather than being removed to a psychiatric hospital, he was sent to prison. On 9 March, nineteen days after this, again due to a series of calamitous decisions, including the stopping of 'special observations' and the removal of his cellmate to attend court, when officers did check his cell they found him hanging by a radio flex. He could not be resuscitated. They discovered a number of suicide notes in his cell.

An inquiry was held into his death eighteen months later, but it appears nothing had changed. Throughout Britain there have been numerous inquiries, but the sad conclusion is that the culture seems in many cases to resemble Mullin's – that suicide is inevitable. I do not think Grant Farquhar thinks this is so; there is much more to his analysis than I have written. Preventing suicide is difficult, but rates vary within different countries' prison systems; real effort should be made to bring the best practice into our service.

There is a final chapter of reflections and thoughts about the subject, but my view is that Alan Mullin was the classical case of an outsider. Throughout history, such people have appeared, disrupted and changed how other people think or behave about the meaning of their lives or the approach to their activities. They are often difficult to know but they usually make a positive contribution to our lives, often, like Alan Mullin, at great cost to themselves and those who love them.

Crazy Sorrow is well illustrated with many outstanding historic colour prints and contains contributions from many other climbers and sources. It is well produced and though highly priced is unlike any other climbing book I have ever read: think Irvine Welsh and *Trainspotting* or Colin Wilson's *The Outsider*. It is a hard read, but it touches on a subject that we all need to know much more about. My recommendation is: despite the sadness and the terrible outcome, do buy and read it!

Crazy Sorrow: the Life and Death of Alan Mullin, Grant Farquhar (ed.) (Dundee: Atlantis Publishing, 2019).

This review first appeared on *Footless Crow* in July 2019

20

HARD ROCK: GREAT BRITISH ROCK CLIMBS FROM VS TO E4

'It's an old Ken Wilson maxim: a picture is worth a thousand words, so snap away, snap away!'

— FROM A SONG BY THE AUTHOR

This is the fourth edition of one of the most influential climbing books of the twentieth century. The first edition appeared in 1974, a second in 1981 and a third in 1992, all compiled by the late Ken Wilson. This new edition, compiled by Ian Parnell, is now appearing in a changed world, heralded in a new century with digital publishing and communication, and a sea-change within the sport of rock climbing, impacted by equipment innovation, the spread in the UK of over 400 indoor climbing walls, and the increasing popularity of sport climbing and bouldering – some might suggest to the detriment of 'trad'.

Hopefully, this new, revamped edition will capture the imagination of the many newcomers emerging in our sport, mainly from indoor climbing, to embrace all that is adventurous and challenging about traditional British rock climbing, set in some of the most beautiful landscapes to be found anywhere.

When a large format *Hard Rock* appeared in 1974, its inception by Ken Wilson is now misreported by some of the pundits. Its origins began on the

Continent, when in 1970 Walter Pause and Jürgen Winkler's *Im extremen fels: 100 kletterführen in den Alpen* ('100 classic extreme climbing routes in the Alps') first appeared. This was an immediate publishing success. A staffer who was something of a climber at the London publisher Hart-Davis, MacGibbon, noted this and phoned Ken Wilson – who was by that time editing *Mountain* magazine – for his views about producing a similar volume of outstanding British climbs. Ken, always a man with strong opinions, retorted it would need to be different here in the UK: a book with essay-type descriptions, literary, with a good photographic cover, highlighting our tradition of bold and self-protected rock climbs, keeping the route and not the climber centre stage. His interlocutor was impressed; Hart-Davis, MacGibbon commissioned Ken to compile such a book. In passing, around the same time there appeared in France *Le Massif du Mont-Blanc: les 100 plus belles courses* ('The Mont Blanc Massif: the 100 finest routes') compiled by Gaston Rébuffat, which was another groundbreaking publication and instant success. But both this and Pause's book were more guidebooks than Wilson's *Hard Rock*.

Life is a succession of accidents: if that phone call had not occurred, then Ken's later publications of *Classic Rock, Extreme Rock* and *Cold Climbs,* all in the same format as *Hard Rock,* might never have appeared. And if he had not been editing *Mountain* magazine, he would hardly have been known to a staffer at a London publishing house.

Not enough credit has been heaped on the historical development of this by recent commentators, for *Mountain* magazine would never have come into existence without its predecessor *Mountain Craft,* the house magazine of the Mountaineering Association. The Mountaineering Association was formed in 1947 by another controversialist, Jerry Wright, and many climbers of the 1950s cut their teeth on MA courses in the UK and the Alps. Ken and a school friend, his early climbing partner Dave Cook, learned their alpine craft on an MA course in Arolla. Allan Austin learned to climb in the 1950s on a beginners' MA course in Llanberis instructed by Robin Collomb. The MA was kept functioning by Jerry Wright, and on his demise it began to unravel. The editor of *Mountain Craft* was a *Guardian* journalist, Roger Redfern, someone I knew from having written articles for him. He was far-seeing, realising that with the winding up of the MA, a buyer had to be found for the magazine. How he settled on Ken is another story, but to Wilson's credit he gave up a secure job in architectural photography in 1968 and took it on, eventually changing its title to *Mountain* and serving as editor from 1969 to 1978.

Those who were never privileged to know Ken Wilson, who died in 2016, missed meeting perhaps one of the most controversial and influential figures of the British mountaineering scene in the last half century. His brusque approach did not always win him friends, but as a climbing publisher he was pre-eminent, and his final effort, a total revamp of *Classic Rock*, published shortly before his death, was his sixtieth publication. There are so many stories surrounding him that I will only give a single illustration of how his character impacted on his fellow climbers. In 1972, he applied to become a member of the Alpine Club, an application which generated a previously unequalled wealth of correspondence. A group of members threatened to resign if he were ever to be elected, but those were offset by those who threatened to resign if he were *not* elected. Happily, he was elected and his scene-setting, original, historic introduction in the new edition of *Hard Rock* is included in full and gives some measure of the man.

This new edition is truly full of high-impact photography, with colour included throughout, but I would have kept a few of the original black and white prints. For instance, Leo Dickinson's picture of Gogarth's *A Dream of White Horses* would have been a must to include for me, as it was for Wilson who, on one occasion in a considered judgement, designated this picture as, 'one of the ten best of all climbing pictures!' Black and white is sometimes more atmospheric, more moody and sharp-edged than colour. The original *Hard Rock* included sixty climbing essays; this new edition has sixty-three, but some of the originals have been dropped, including Kilnsey's *Main Overhang* and *The Scoop* at Strone Ulladale, the first written by Dave Nicol, the second by Doug Scott. However, their essays appear at the end of the book as an addendum; they were removed on the grounds of being climbs outside the high-standard free climb grades of this volume. Two other originals which have also been axed really hurt, for one is the *North Crag Eliminate* of Castle Rock of Triermain, pioneered in 1952 by Harold Drasdo and me (I was sixteen years old at the time), and *Deer Bield Buttress*, Arthur Dolphin's masterful 1951 climb, the essay for which was also by Harold, one of the best in the original book. Both routes have now fallen down!

The original essays were by some of the then best-known personalities of the British climbing world, including Hamish MacInnes, Pete Crew,

Chris Bonington, Ed Ward Drummond, Al Alvarez, Ian McNaught-Davis, Jim Perrin and Allan Austin, but it was some of the lesser-known people in 1974 who for me wrote some of the most memorable pieces, for example Dave Cook on the *North-West Girdle* at Almscliff and Robin Campbell writing about *Swastika* on the Etive Slabs. Other standout originals were Royal Robbins on *A Dream of White Horses* and Jimmy Marshall on *Carnivore*, the first because it is about an ascent Royal made of the climb while partnered by Ken Wilson: he captured his character very well in his witty but kindly writing. Then Jimmy Marshall's because it was such a breakthrough Scottish climb in which Jimmy wrote how Pat Walsh presented him with his piton hammer, left hanging by Jimmy off a retreat peg after he had made a second attempt on the route. I partnered Pat on the occasion when we actually succeeded. I hasten to add that Jimmy soon returned, and he too finished the route. In passing (once more), in the late 1950s, Walsh was among the most outstanding rock climbers in the UK.

One of the great climbs in *Hard Rock* is *Shibboleth*, Robin Smith's route on the Slime Wall of the Buachaille Etive Mòr. Pat had opened up that feature long before Robin, and he felt you could climb it almost anywhere! At a desperate standard, Joe 'Morty' Smith and I experienced real difficulties while attempting to repeat his climbs, as his verbal descriptions were so vague.

The routes included in this new edition stretch across the Scottish Highlands and Islands (including the Old Man of Hoy and Pabbay), the Lake District, the Pennines and Peak, North and South Wales, even down to South-West England; the climbs chosen include mountain walls, gritstone outcrops and some epic sea-cliff adventures. The book includes thirteen routes and essays by nine new authors, some at a higher grade than the earlier editions, probably aimed at the 'trad' connoisseurs' range of VS to E2. I think these would be within the capabilities of a majority of climbers, but E3 or E4 has to be a maybe, unless there has been a vast grade swing upwards in the last decade.

Of the new authors, a couple really did grab me. First, Dave Pickford's essay about Swanage and two climbs at the Boulder Ruckle, including *Mars* by an old mate, Richard Crewe. I had the 'grip' of pioneering a new route with Richard on that cliff; our equipment included peg hammers with curved picks to climb out of the last section of loose ground to the finish. The second, Kevin Howett writing about the *Vulcan Wall* on Skye.

Originally pioneered by another old mate, Ian Clough, and Hamish MacInnes. The latter I first met on the Cobbler in 1951 as a fifteen-year-old.

For me, the whole book is a climb along memory lane; so many friends from the original have now departed the scene. Re-reading about their great climbs – Whillans on *Extol*, Pete Biven on *Moonraker*, Dolphin on *Kipling Groove*, Tony Barley on *Carnage* and Nat Allen writing about Peak classics like the *Chee Tor Girdle* (I lived at Nat's mother's house in Derby for three and a half years) – brought them back in their pomp for me. One figure resplendent who remains with us is the Baron, Joe Brown.* I speak to him regularly by phone, but I can guess anyone reading *Hard Rock* and coming new into the sport must think: how could one climber pioneer so many of the most outstanding rock climbs in this country? The 1950s were his decade, and the 1960s almost the same; in no other sport do I know where one participant has been such an influence for such a long period. We both agree that to be active in those decades was indeed a happy accident of birth.

Being a pedant, I feel I need to provide some further information for Frank Cannings, who wrote the essay about *Suicide Wall* and *Bow Wall* on Bosigran in Cornwall. He was correct that on the first ascent on the crux pitch of the first route, Peter Biven stood on Trevor Peck's head and placed a peg for aid to gain a pair of cracks leading up to the next stance. He also mentions in his article that the Rock and Ice Club visited Cornwall in 1957. On that visit, Joe Brown and I were guided on occasion by Biven and Peck and we all four made the third ascent of *Suicide Wall*. Joe led the route, including the crux, free, then Peter and Trevor joined our rope, not wishing to try to emulate Brown's free lead of the crux. So, Brown led the first free ascent of *Suicide Wall*. Readers may be interested to know that I had been to Cornwall in 1956 and met on that occasion a very ancient A.W. Andrews, who is acknowledged as the original pioneer of sea cliff climbing in this country. My waywardness in spending my precious holiday time climbing in an area such as West Penwith was met with scorn by Don Whillans. 'You should save climbing in such areas until you're old and past it!' he advised, when we agreed to go to Cornwall in 1957; Don was heading for Masherbrum!

---

* Ed: Joe passed away in April 2020, the month after this review was published.

Ian Parnell on Kedar Dome (6,831 metres), Gangotri. © Tim Emmett

I noted in Cannings' article that he seemed surprised that we did not achieve more on our visit, but in those days we all worked and enjoyed restricted holidays. A week in Cornwall was as much as most could manage. Joe by then had his own one-man property repair business, so he could afford to stay on after we left. He pioneered the first section of *Bow Wall* but could not find anyone to second him up the rest of that route.

All in all, this *Hard Rock* is a worthy successor to all that has gone before. I can imagine Ken Wilson looking at this from on high and doubtless he would have something to add on incorporating some ideas into the new edition of the book. It is fitting that Ian Parnell has taken this on, for I would guess that in Ken's eyes he would be a 'real' climber, with many different disciplines under his belt: of bold and badly protected leads on British cliffs, a pioneer of Scottish winter routes, an ascent of the north face of the Eiger and outstanding success in the Himalaya. Wilson would have revelled in that.

Finally, the book's layout and quality are what we have come to expect of Vertebrate. The line drawing endpapers by Malc Baxter add to the whole excellent appearance of the work. But as a tightwad I am wondering if the price of £39.95 is one that will put it out of reach of most of the young and or the impecunious. However, maybe a case might be made that in view of the dreaded coronavirus, a grant to purchase might be forthcoming from the DHSS to help any such activist to while away their boredom while in self-imposed isolation.

Hard Rock: Great British Rock Climbs from VS to E4, Ian Parnell (ed.) (Sheffield: Vertebrate Publishing, 2020).

This review first appeared on *Footless Crow* in March 2020.

21

A'CHREAG DHEARG: CLIMBING STORIES OF THE ANGUS GLENS

'They shattered the spell of the mighty Dr Bell, they were all good men and true.'

— FROM A SONG BY TOM PATEY

When I lived in Scotland in the 1960s, the southern aspect of the Cairngorm massif was hardly known to my Edinburgh companions in the Squirrels. Although I used to go to Dundee regularly on business, climbing on the Arbroath sea cliffs on occasion en route, I had not then heard of the climbing revolution that was under way in the Angus Glens. (I stayed in nearby Broughty Ferry, where the big attraction was the folk club, highlighting Ewan MacColl, whom I was to learn later came from Salford where he was known as Jimmie Miller.)

This book, compiled by Grant Farquhar, is revelatory and was a joy to read by this old timer. The first articles in this compilation illustrate the story of the area, that Dundee used to be the centre of the manufacturing of jute, and that in the First World War its denizens were very much the recruiting city of the Black Watch regiment, which suffered many deaths and injuries.

*Grant Farquhar making the third ascent of Colder than a Hooker's Heart at
Creag Dubh in 1988. © Graeme Ettle*

We also learn a little of the family history of the compiler of this
volume, a local boy, a Dundonian who now resides in Bermuda but who
has a track record of difficult ascents across the UK, with an equally
impressive CV as a climbing writer.

Also, surprisingly related in this book, there was one of the first access
battles, when the regular route all the way to Ballater and Braemar from Forfar
– the name by which the whole Angus region used to be known – was blocked
by the landowner. This ended in the Court of Session in Edinburgh when the
claimants won one of the most important cases in the history of the outdoor
movement. This was known as the battle for Jock's Road, so well recounted by
Des Hannigan, a local climber who made his name further south on the
Cornish sea cliffs. In January 1959, a terrible tragedy occurred on Jock's Road
from Braemar to Glen Doll, a distance of over eighteen miles and which goes
above the 3,000-foot contour, when a party of five became lost in worsening
conditions and eventually perished. There was extensive publicity at the time
and it led to the present mountain rescue unit being established in the district.

The early mountaineering in the area was at the initiative of the Scottish Mountaineering Club (SMC). Meets were held at the home of Sir Hugh Munro (a baronet, no less), whose family seat was near Kirriemuir and whose name is now so aligned with his list of peaks in Scotland above 3,000 feet, first published in the SMC journal in 1891. There is a photograph in the book of a five-strong party roped together in winter conditions on the Angus hills. While global warming is affecting our winters now, in the latter years of the nineteenth century the snow and ice could be counted on by these stalwarts. Another famous figure who lived close by was J.M. Barrie, author of the Peter Pan stories; although he was not a climber, quotes from his work inevitably appear with some regularity in this book.

One of the outstanding pioneers to emerge from this area was J.H.B. Bell, who pioneered some of the great climbs on Ben Nevis, besides local classics in the Angus Glens like *Maud Buttress*. He was also a writer of some distinction. I can remember how his book *Bell's Scottish Climbs*, published by Gollancz, was well received when it appeared in 1988.

And so the scene is set for what must have been one of the most action-packed groups to emerge from a big city to find their way into climbing, winter or summer. A group of teenagers, none of whom had been on any kind of course, who came into the sport by a traditional way: they learned from their mistakes. From the first, they were keen to explore and to try new routes, but most of all were there to enjoy themselves and find out where the boundaries were to their lives. They came together and, tongue in cheek, called themselves the 'Men of Steel'. Many appear in the text only by their nicknames: Dr Evil (Grant), Pot, Hendo, and so on. One without a nickname but one of the keenest new routers was Simon Stewart. In his writings, he claims that he was never the best climber of the group, but his new routes on the cliffs of Glen Clova bear witness to his abilities at the time.

They based themselves in the Carn Dearg Mountaineering Club hut in Glen Clova and became regulars at the pub in the valley. This was in the mid-1980s, and illustrates how much climbing has now changed with the popularity of indoor walls, diets, training, fitness, strength and speed. At a later date, some of the Men of Steel found places in Dundee, buildings they could climb on, notably the walls of the engineering department of the university, but they were probably among the last groups to find out what climbing was all about by themselves.

We are brought up short by the chapter on the 'Life of Reilly'. This tells the story of the twins, Ged and Ian Reilly. At this time, some of the Angus climbers were travelling further afield. On 21 January 1978, Ian Reilly and nineteen-year-old Brian Simpson fell off a route in the inner corrie of Creag Meagaidh. Ged, who was in the area on that day, went looking for his brother and his companion. By the time they were found, it was too late: both had succumbed to their injuries and the cold. Ged, despite this terrible accident, still climbs.

In a book of such length there is only space to concentrate on articles that give the feeling of the work, so I will only highlight those which I think were typical of the whole. The first is by Grant Farquhar himself and is titled, 'The Pale Rider'. It goes out on a limb in deciding how dangerous climbing really is. This thoughtful article had its genesis in an email from Simon Stewart. In that, he noted that the three most experienced and oldest climbers whom he had ever climbed with – Andy Nisbet, Martin Moran and Doug Lang – had all died at advanced ages in climbing accidents. This posited the question: do climbers become more at risk as they grow old?

Grant is a psychiatrist, so well able to pontificate on risk taking. He comes to the conclusion that climbing is not as dangerous as some would believe; other activities like base jumping, for instance, are much more so. As someone who gave some lectures on this subject I would say that there are now different levels of risk involved in the activities. Sport climbing should be safe, trad rock climbing less so, winter climbing even less so, with the most dangerous being greater range mountaineering, with the Himalayan variety being the most demanding in this respect. Freud inevitably is included in Farquhar's musings, with libido, the sex drive and *Thanatos,* the death wish, mentioned. His conclusion that we are all going to die in any case is true, and though most of us try to avoid facing up to this, his advice is to enjoy our lives and to get out climbing.

This leads on, under the title 'Redemption on Creag Death', to the terrible accident on Creag Dubh which befell Simon Stewart in the early part of 1987. Pushing his grades, he set out on a route on the main wall, *Acapulco,* a badly protected E4. When I lived in Edinburgh Creag Dubh was a favourite haunt of the Squirrels. One winter, Bugs McKeith and I even soloed the frozen watercourse which splits the crag, and with Dave Bathgate I made one or two first ascents. It is a difficult cliff, protection-wise, and unfortunately when Stewart fell off *Acapulco*, what gear he had, pulled; he hit the ground and was badly injured. Fortunately, a mountain rescue team was training nearby, and he was lifted by chopper to Raigmore Hospital in Inverness, somewhere that has poignant memories for me for it was where I first met my future wife, who had been on her way to ski in the Cairngorms when she was involved in a road accident.

It was to be thirty years before Simon climbed again. The accident resulted in him concentrating on his university studies and, much to the surprise of his lecturers, he became an outstanding student which led him eventually to becoming a professor. Much of his early climbing and first ascents were with a fellow student, Cathy. In 1992, his reverie was to be interrupted by a call from fellow Men of Steel member Graeme Ettle, informing him that Cathy had died in the Himalaya.

The final article I would like to highlight is by Sophie Grace Chappell on the naming of climbs. Many climbers have previously pointed out that they rely on tradition, others on events, or features, like *The White Slab* on Cloggy. Some climbers, like Harold Drasdo, often used historical names. But Sophie has an unusual take on this with the titles of many pop and wider musical pieces, even old music-hall favourites. How climbs are named is often the source of much discussion: usually it is up to those making the first ascent to do this, but in the case of Glen Clova it is revealed in this book that many of the new routes are named in keeping with already existing challenges.

The main text is rounded off with a poem by Sophie in memory of Andy Nisbet and Steve Perry, two leading Scottish mountaineers who died on Ben Hope in February 2019. The book then concludes with a list of the sources from where some of the articles originate. The work involved in putting together such a compilation is impressive, and Grant Farquhar is to be complimented on that.

All profits from sales go to the Scottish Mountaineering Trust, a charity which gives grants to organisations that promote recreation, knowledge and safety in the mountains, especially the mountains of Scotland.

A'Chreag Dhearg: Climbing Stories of the Angus Glens, Grant Farquhar (ed.) (Edinburgh: Scottish Mountaineering Press, 2021).

This review first appeared on *Footless Crow* in February 2022.

ACKNOWLEDGEMENTS

The author would like to record his sincere thanks for the memory of the late John Appleby, founder and webmaster of *Footless Crow*. *footlesscrow. blogspot.com*

The author would also like to thank: Christine Baxter-Jones for the photo of Roger Baxter-Jones; Adam Butterworth, editor of the *Alpine Journal*; Leo Dickinson for his photo portrait of Don Whillans; Ed Douglas, for his editing of the originals of the Falak Sar, Joe Brown and Don Whillans articles in the *Alpine Journal*; Tim Emmett for his photo of Ian Parnell; Graham Ettle for his photo of Grant Farquhar; Sue Hare, photo sales manager at the Alpine Club; Bernie Ingrams, honorary keeper of the Alpine Club's photographs; Andy Kirkpatrick for his portrait photo; Bernadette McDonald for her assistance in tracing some photos; Tamara Robbins for the photo of her father, Royal Robbins, and David Smart for his help in providing the Royal Robbins portrait; Bob A. Schelfhout-Aubertijn for his assistance in tracing some photos; Connie Self, Jeff's Lowe's *Metanoia* and the Jeff Lowe Mountain Foundation for the portrait of Jeff Lowe; John Stainforth for his photo of John Syrett.